EURRGH!

IS IT JUST ME OR
IS EUROPE MERDE?

Constable & Robinson Ltd
55–56 Russell Square
London WC1B 4HP
www.constablerobinson.com

First published in the UK by Constable,
an imprint of Constable & Robinson Ltd, 2013

Copyright © Mark Leigh 2013

A copy of the British Library Cataloguing in Publication Data
is available from the British Library

ISBN 978-1-47210-929-3 (hardback)
ISBN 978-1-47210-940-8 (ebook)

Printed and bound in the UK

10 9 8 7 6 5 4 3 2 1

EURRGH!
IS IT JUST ME OR
IS EUROPE MERDE?

MARK LEIGH

CONSTABLE

CONTENTS

CONTENTS

DISCLAIMER

ALTHOUGH ALL THE basic information and visitor attractions contained in this book are factual, the aberrant prejudices, irrational bigotry and unrelenting contempt expressed belong solely to the author and definitely do not reflect the views of the publisher. Not only that, but the accuracy of his so-called translations is risible. Quite frankly we should have never agreed to this book in the first place but by the time we realised what it would be like, we'd already commissioned it, and he said that if we rescinded his contract he'd haul us before the European Court of Human Rights. Talk about bloody irony!

I don't hold with abroad and think that foreigners
speak English when our backs are turned.
Quentin Crisp

INTRODUCTION

When in Rome, don't do what the Romans do ... don't even go

INTRODUCTION

When in Rome, don't do what the Romans do ... don't even go

THINK OF THIS less as a guide book and more as a warning; the last time Great Britain went into Europe with any degree of success was on 6 June 1944 and since then things have gone rapidly downhill faster than you can say 'Veto'.

The UK's mistrust of, and disenchantment with, Europe is at an all-time high. In fact the only people who actually care about this landmass are overpaid MEPs and their staff who ride the EU gravy train (or as they say, 'le train de sauce'). Even the most passionate of Europhiles realise that the word 'Europe' has so many negative associations that they call it 'The Continent' and promote the notion of 'ooh-la-la' to try to make it seem more exotic and appealing. However, this ploy doesn't work either, as the word 'continental' is always associated with inferior cold breakfasts; likewise, 'ooh-la-la' is supposed to conjure up images of saucy French maids whereas the reality of European 'sexiness' is obese, oiled-up, bald businessmen wearing Speedos and women with an aversion to shaving.

EUrrgh! exposes these and hundreds of other lies and misconceptions about Europe; not just about the conniving, treacherous EU but the countries themselves and what's wrong, repellent and laughable about their people, customs, cuisine and so-called 'attractions'.

There are those, of course, who promote Europe as a great big cultural melting pot – a metaphor used to symbolise different ingredients mixing and fusing together to form a harmonious whole. What they don't realise is that one of the consequences of a melting pot is that there will naturally be a scum on the surface. That's the French.

Mark Leigh, Surrey, England 2013

PS For the purposes of this book Europe consists of the twenty-six countries currently in the EU, obviously excluding the UK and Ireland. This means I've left out places like Andorra, Belarus, Kosovo, Liechtenstein, Moldova and a few others. To be honest, these places don't really count for anything and are basically just irritating pimples on the spotty backside of the European mainland.

SO, YOU THINK YOU'RE
A XENOPHOBE . . .

XENOPHOBE . . . **IT'S IRONIC** that even the word that means someone who dislikes or fears foreign customs, behaviour or foreigners themselves is actually foreign. If I were paranoid (and I'm not … who's been saying I am?), I'd say the introduction of this word into our language is further proof of Johnny Foreigner infiltrating our culture, trying to destroy it from within.

The following simple yet very scientific test will indicate whether you're a bona fide xenophobe (my god … there's another two foreign words creeping in … they're bloody everywhere!)

Anyway, tick the boxes if you agree with these statements:

❶ Does hearing someone speak English with a European accent instinctively make you think 'spy' rather than tourist?

❷ Does reading the following words make you feel uncomfortable and anxious: smorgasbord, fettuccine, maelstrom, zeitgeist, jalapeño, abattoir, Luftwaffe?

❸ Do you believe that foreigners are over here to steal your job and your partner rather than just go on the London Eye or watch the changing of the guard?

❹ If you hear someone talking in a different language do you automatically presume they're talking about you? And not in a good way?

⑤ When discussing foreign food do you automatically replace the word 'cuisine' with the word 'muck'? ☐

⑥ If you're walking home at night and hear footsteps behind you do you automatically assume it's Gerard Depardieu? ☐

⑦ Does the presence of two small dots above a letter, or an O with a diagonal line through it make you want to scream or punch someone really hard? ☐

⑧ Do you think people wearing berets are members of a dark, insidious cult? ☐

⑨ When you hear the words 'European unity' is your first thought an invasion by stormtroopers rather than the establishment of a free market and common laws to combat social exclusion and discrimination? ☐

⑩ Do you blame your poor sexual performance on your anxiety about being able to live up to the reputations of the Italians, Spanish and French as better lovers? ☐

⑪ When you see subtitled speech on a foreign film do you think, 'I wonder what they're *really* saying?' ☐

⑫ Do you instinctively feel morally superior to anyone wearing clogs? ☐

RESULTS

★ **10–12** Congratulations! As Darth Vader might have said, 'The xenophobe is strong in this one.' You're the sort of person whose dream holiday would involve a) a long weekend in Paris, b) total immunity from prosecution and c) a baseball bat.

★ **6–9** Not bad. You're obviously someone who agrees with Nancy Mitford, who said, '… abroad is unutterably bloody and foreigners are fiends'. Keep up the prejudice and intolerance.

★ **5 or less** Shame on you! Don't you realise it's completely natural to distrust anyone who's not British? After all, it's not just a coincidence that nearly all of the major wars since history began have involved foreigners.

FIFTY-ONE REASONS
TO HATE EUROPE

THE MAIN REASON to hate Europe of course, is the EU, a grotesque, totalitarian, officious, unaccountable, corrupt money-sucking machine that costs the UK over £50,000,000 each day and which devours national sovereignty and pukes out unwanted, unwelcome and intrusive legislation – however, there are many other grounds to hate this entire continent:

1. Shops that open at 10 a.m. and close at 4 p.m. – with a two-hour lunch break in between
2. Oompah bands
3. Restaurant staff with the manners of a gibbon and the sense of urgency of a sloth
4. Parisians
5. Police forces who are the bastard offspring of the Gestapo and the Stasi
6. Countries for whom the word 'mañana' conveys a sense of urgency
7. National costumes that are as preposterous as they are pointless
8. Taxi journeys where the meters go faster than the cab
9. Yodelling
10. £6 cups of coffee
11. Tintin
12. The metric system
13. Quiche Lorraine
14. Brussels sprouts
15. Bouzouki music

16. Hordes of foreign students with acne resembling the surface of a small asteroid and backpacks the size of Andorra

17. Street signs that are a homage to small typography rather than acting as a helpful guide to your location

18. Topo Gigio

19. Asterix the Gaul

20. City centres infested with hordes of cyclists who change direction and speed with even more unpredictability than Chaos Theory

21. Donkey abuse

22. Football teams with stupid names like the Zurich Grasshoppers and the Young Boys Bern (who, incidentally, are based in the Swiss town of Wankdorf).

23. Drivers who view speed limits as targets rather than warnings

24. Accordions

25. Feta cheese

26. Beer with the strength of diluted Fanta

27. Lederhosen

28. A history of brutal tyrannical despots (Vlad the Impaler, Torquemada, Hitler, General Franco and Angela Merkel)

29. Women who subscribe to the misguided idea that armpit hair is alluring

30. The twenty-four-hour clock

31. Food where the core ingredient is offal

32. Mime (not so much an art form as a sign of mental illness)

33. The Smurfs

34. Levels of bureaucracy that would astound even Kafka

35. Small yappy dogs being walked by small yappy owners

36. Feeling like a clown after discovering your shoes are size 44

37. Cobbled old towns that confuse the word 'quaint' with 'over-commercialised tourist traps'

38. The locals' insistence of communicating just by shrugging and waving their arms about

39. Butter mountains and milk lakes (not a good place to visit if you're lactose intolerant)
40. The use of a comma as a decimal point
41. Regulations that determine the acceptable shape of a banana
42. German Measles
43. Norwegian whaling
44. Polish spelling
45. Eurodisco
46. Eurozone
47. Eurotrash
48. Eurovision
49. Anything else preceded by the word 'Euro' (apart from Euro sceptic)
50. The Vengaboys
51. The Cheeky Girls

What else is Europe but a conglomeration of mistakes?
Hans Enzenberger

AUSTRIA

No one clings to former glories as the Austrians do, and since these former glories include one of the most distasteful interludes in history, this is not their most attractive feature.

Bill Bryson

NCE HIDEOUSLY WEALTHY and the epicentre of the mighty Habsburg Empire that extended across much of Europe, modern Austria is now a mere shadow of its former self; a neutered, neutral, inward-looking country. Back in the day, Austria's most illustrious sons included Wolfgang Amadeus Mozart, Johann Strauss, Franz Schubert, Alfred Adler, Sigmund Freud and Gustav Klimt; in more recent years the country has spawned Adolf Hitler, Arnold Schwarzenegger and Josef Fritzl. In a similar vein, historic Austrian inventions have included psychoanalysis, the waltz, the sewing machine and the Pulitzer Prize. In modern times its contributions have been limited to the Glock semi-automatic pistol and the Pez dispenser.

Austria today tries to put a brave face on its changed fortunes. Publicly it promotes itself as a small nation with a big past. However, the reality is that it's the Miss Havisham of Europe; bitter, twisted and full of resentment – not just for the passing of its glory days but because of its lingering reputation as the Nazi Party's most heinous collaborator. It's a country that takes its frustrations out on visitors by offering over-hyped and overpriced tourist attractions, arrogant locals who pretend not to understand a word of English and a service culture where even being 'adequate' is seen as going above and beyond the call of duty.

Many Austrians demonstrate a stubborn refusal to acknowledge their country's spectacular fall from grace and firmly believe their nation still has a role on the world stage. It does – except nowadays that role is just operating the curtains or moving scenery about.

DID YOU KNOW?

★ The first postcards were invented in Austria in 1869, presumably so visitors could write home and say how disappointed and unhappy they were.

★ There is a village called Fucking twenty-one miles north of Saltzburg. The locals are called Fuckingers.

★ Despite its great musical legacy the most famous Austrian musician nowadays is a drummer who played with B*Witched and Geri Halliwell.

VIENNA

Spend some time in Vienna and you'll understand that when Midge Ure sang, 'It means nothing me,' he was absolutely correct. The trouble is that the Viennese treat their city as if it's New York, London or Tokyo; dynamic, vibrant and thriving … whereas in reality it's like its baroque architecture: ornate and over-elaborate but at its core, pompous, superficial and just impressive for its own sake. If the city was a person it would be suffering from massive delusions of grandeur and would require extensive therapy – a delicious irony when you consider Vienna is the home of psychoanalysis.

Attractions to avoid

★ **Hofburg Palace** Until 1918 this was the residence of the Emperor of Austria; now it houses three museums that provide an insight into the everyday life of the imperial court. One of these museums contains the Imperial Silver Collection and a comprehensive range of tableware and other utensils. Fans of historic cutlery will not be disappointed; everyone else will be.

★ **Spanish Riding School** Most guidebooks say that the dressage displays put on by the white Lipizzaner stallions will enchant spectators. It's difficult to see how sad-looking, lethargic horses prancing around in a circle or being whipped so they momentarily rear up on their hind legs can be considered 'enchanting' in any sense of the word. Buying admission tickets here is likely to be one of the worst-value purchases of your entire life.

★ **Stephansplatz** This is a square in the geographical centre of Vienna and named after Vienna's most prominent building, the gothic St Stephen's Cathedral. You can do three things at Stephansplatz; stare at the church, go shopping in exceptionally expensive stores or eat at exceptionally expensive cafés. Expect to have to fight your way through a mad scrum of tourists, more tourists, even more tourists and annoying men wearing cheesy Mozart costumes and wigs trying to sell tickets for overpriced classical concerts.

MOZART: MUSICAL GENIUS OR PERVERT?

Mozart would write letters full of references to excrement to his relatives and one of his musical compositions, a canon in B-flat major for six voices, was entitled 'Leck mich im Arsch' which translates as 'Lick me in the arse'.

FIVE ABSOLUTELY TRUE FACTS ABOUT AUSTRIA
(NONE OF WHICH WILL INSPIRE YOU TO VISIT)

★ Approximately half of Austrian men are overweight, the highest rate in the EU.

★ Among men, the country has one of the lower incidences of hand washing after toilet use.

★ A recent survey showed that one in ten young people thought Adolf Hitler was 'not all bad'.

★ You have to pay for tap water in most restaurants.

★ It's now a criminal offence to make blonde jokes (punishable by up to two years in prison).

Other places in Austria to avoid

SALZBURG

Located at the edge of the Alps, Salzburg is most famous for its musical diversity; this is the city that gave the world both Mozart and *The Sound of Music*.

★ **For Mozart fans:** You can see where he was born (the Mozart Geburtshaus) and where he lived (the Mozart Wohnhaus) but both attractions are shockingly poor, mainly containing facsimiles and reproductions of portraits, musical instruments and manuscripts, the real items being housed in different (i.e. better) museums around the world. The Geburtshaus does however contain some of Mozart's hair and one of his buttons. Supposedly.

★ **For *The Sound of Music* fans:** There are countless *Sound of Music* tours that let you follow in the footsteps of the movie and the real Von Trapp family. These tours usually entail cramming an old minivan with as many people as possible and driving at speed past various film locations while an indifferent guide shouts an ill-informed commentary in a thick German accent that's so incomprehensible he might be talking about Julie Andrews ... then again he might not. After experiencing this tour you too will want to escape over the mountains to Switzerland on foot. Less von Trapp than Tourist Trapp.

Useful Austrian phrases

★ I just wanted directions to the station, not your extremist views on politics, religion and race.
Ich wollte nur Richtungen zum Bahnhof, nicht Ihre extremistischen Ansichten über Politik, Religion und Rasse.

★ Thank you for your suggestion that I should buy lederhosen and a hat with a feather in it, but I will settle for a souvenir fridge magnet.
Vielen Dank für Ihren Vorschlag, ich solle Lederhosen und Hut mit einer Feder in es zu kaufen, aber ich werde für ein Erinnerungsfoto Kühlschrankmagnet begleichen.

★ Not only do you not understand the phrase 'The customer is always right', you have absolutely no concept of the word 'customer'.
Sie verstehen nicht, den Satz: 'Der Kunde hat immer Recht.' Zusätzlich haben Sie absolut keine Vorstellung von dem Wort 'Kunde'.

Five reasons you know you're in Austria

❶ **Beer is everywhere** You can buy beer in coffee shops and even McDonald's; it's said that beer flows like water in Austria (and in many cases, tastes like it).

❷ **... and so are dogs** Austrians have a different understanding of the word hygiene; dogs are welcome in most places including cinemas, shops, hairdressers, bars and even cafés and restaurants.

❸ **You'll be coughing** Smoking is rife in Austria with about half of all adults lighting up. Locals seem oblivious to the term 'passive smoking' or why blowing smoke in your face might actually be considered anti-social.

❹ **Pessimism is as natural as breathing (or coughing)** Demonstrating the same positive mental attitude as Eeyore, Austrians love nothing better than to criticise, moan and complain about everything in the most negative way. Regardless of the topic under discussion Austrians will think that it's terrible/shocking/shameful or just plain bad.

❺ **The locals say what they really mean** You'll find that Austrians don't pussyfoot around when it comes to telling you what they think. They call it being 'honest'; you'll call it being 'aggressively hostile'.

BELGIUM

Belgium is a nice place, though. It's the place people go to when they're on their way to another place, a place they're going to spend more time at. It's kind of the Jennifer Aniston of countries.

Craig Ferguson

THE BELGIUM TOURIST Office realises the country has a major image problem and vehemently disputes the fact that it's mind-numbingly boring; instead it tries to put a bit of spin on the situation by calling Belgium 'Europe's most eccentric country'. If eccentric means dreary, they are indeed correct, but don't just take my word for it. The fact that *famousbelgians.net* even exists shows that Belgians are very aware of their country's reputation and will try anything to overcome what they call 'gross misconceptions'. A quick look at this website shows that the famous Belgians listed include Edward de Smedt (the inventor of asphalt), Ernest Solvay (the man behind the process for extracting sodium carbonate from brine) and Walter Arfeuille (some bloke who lifted 281.5 kg 17 cm off the ground with his teeth). To make up the numbers the website also includes Hercule Poirot – and he's not even real.

Museums here, which can often be a window into the soul of a country, let alone somewhere to get out of the rain, are equally lacklustre and uninspiring, with whole buildings in Belgium dedicated to the history of woollen clothing manufacture, crystals, French fries, brewery trucks, rural trams, masks, lace and artificial lighting (yes, really).

Historically, Belgium was known as one of the Low Countries. This has nothing to do with the height of its land above sea level, and everything to do with what your expectations need to be, in order to avoid disappointment.

BELGIUM AND THE CONTEMPORARY ARTS

Belgium has made two contributions to modern culture:
a) The Smurfs
b) Tintin
No more needs to be said.

BRUSSELS

Capital cities are meant to be exciting, dynamic and vibrant: a showcase of a nation's history and its contribution to the fields of art and culture. Given Belgium's reputation it shouldn't surprise you to learn that Brussels is actually best known as being the unofficial capital of the EU, the world's biggest, most tiresome, faceless, dull and loathsome bureaucracy.

Attractions to avoid

★ **The Manneken Pis fountain** Rio de Janeiro has its 99-foot tall Christ the Redeemer, New York has its 150-foot Statue of Liberty, London has its 170-foot Nelson's Column. Even Baghdad had that 40-foot statue of Saddam Hussein before it toppled over. The most famous statue in Belgium's capital is the 2-foot bronze sculpture of a urinating boy. It represents what most visitors feel about this dismal city.

★ **The Parliamentarium** This is the visitor's centre of the European Parliament and, despite having an obscene promotional budget, fails dismally to sound at all interesting. According to its website the best come-ons it can offer are 'The history of European integration using 150 iconic images and historic documents' and an 'innovative and entertaining role-play game to see what it's like to be an MEP'. Admission is free but you'll still feel short-changed.

★ **Atomium** If you ever want to see what a unit cell of an iron crystal magnified 165 million times looks like, then this is it. If you want to pay to venture inside this relic from the 1958 World Fair you'll see various exhibits on absolutely nothing that will hold your interest. Reactions to this landmark vary from 'exceedingly disappointing' to 'why?'

TINTIN

Great Britain gave the world Chaucer, Shakespeare, Dickens, Wordsworth, Tennyson, Hardy, Blake, the Brontës, Tolkien, Austen, Keats, Coleridge, Eliot, Carroll, Wilde, Du Maurier and Orwell. Belgium's contribution to literature is Hergé, creator of Tintin.

Adored and revered in Europe but despised or ignored everywhere else, Tintin books are as dull and long-winded as Brussels' bureaucracy. It won't come as a surprise to learn that the three most exciting Tintin books are *Tintin Goes To The Library* (1942), *Tintin Opens A Window* (1938) and *Tintin Stays In Bed* (1954).

ANTWERP

Best known for its medieval and baroque architecture and as a world-famous diamond centre, the Antwerp tourist office is keen to promote Belgium's second largest city to younger visitors by positioning it as the country's 'capital of cool' and 'home to the trendiest club scene around'. They say that a visit here is like being at one huge party. What they fail to explain is that it's like an office party ... one where you're surrounded by unattractive middle-aged men and women in paper hats who look less like colleagues and more like care-in-the-community patients.

Attractions to avoid

★ **The Diamond Museum (now relocated at the Museum aan de Stroom)** Don't be fooled by the name of this tourist attraction. It's not somewhere constructed solely out of diamonds (which would be mildly interesting), but just a museum dedicated to the story of diamond mining, cutting and polishing. Here you can learn what it takes to make diamonds brilliantly sparkling … the polar opposite of your experience.

★ **Grote Markt** Look beyond the inevitable medieval architecture and you'll see Antwerp's Great Market Square is a depository for beer cans, a home to souvenir stands which make pound shops look classy and a selection of overpriced restaurants fronted by obnoxious, pushy touts. Even the briefest of visits will make you realise that the 'e' at the end of 'Grote' is silent.

DID YOU KNOW?

Belgium has actual towns called Labia, Minge and Spurt.

BRUGES

Another semi-preserved town trying desperately to cling to its former glories, Bruges is famous for beer, lace and the sheer number of underwhelming attractions it is home to. It's no coincidence that the Groeninge Museum here contains 'The Last Judgement' by Hieronymus Bosch. Most of this painting depicts an earth ending by fire, a place where demons seize souls and where the wicked are punished in hell. That's what a long weekend in Bruges feels like.

FIVE ABSOLUTELY TRUE FACTS ABOUT BELGIUM
(NONE OF WHICH WILL INSPIRE YOU TO VISIT)

★ Belgium has three official languages, Dutch, French and German, so there's three times the likelihood of not being understood.

★ Belgium is known as the 'Battleground of Europe' due to the many battles fought in this region (warring nations chose this region as they wanted to fight somewhere that 'didn't matter').

★ Belgium produces 220,000 tons of fattening chocolate per year. It can't be a coincidence that it was a Belgian scientist, Lambert Adolphe Quetelet, who invented the concept of measuring body mass index.

★ You'll be encouraged by locals to try the popular Belgian food Pêches au thon/Perziken met tonijn: halved peaches stuffed with a mixture of tuna and mayonnaise.

★ In Antwerp it's illegal to walk down the main street while wearing a red hat.

Attractions to avoid

★ **Choco-Story: The Chocolate Museum** Take the worst school trip and magnify that tenfold. Add in a generous amount of ennui and a dollop of tedium. Mix until disappointed; that's the recipe for Bruges' chocolate museum. The concept sounds great but endless wall displays about the Mayans and cocoa beans, the role of chocolate among European nobility and the chance to watch a praline being made do not make for an exciting or thought-provoking experience.

★ **The Frietmuseum** This attraction promotes itself as the only museum in the world entirely dedicated to potato fries. After traipsing through exhibits on the history of the potato or viewing a selection of deep-fat fryers, you'll know why.

★ **Bruges railway station** The fact that this is even promoted as an official tourist attraction gives you an indication of the paucity of things to do in Bruges. The best things the Bruges tourist office can say about it are that it's easy to find and that it has a large taxi rank.

USEFUL BELGIAN PHRASES

(Although 60% of the population speak Dutch, French is the preferred language in Brussels. This means that visitors have to remember crucial differences, such as the fact that despite a complete lack of a penis, a sandwich is masculine.)

★ I'd like to book an earlier return flight. Your country has sucked all the happiness out of me.
   Je voudrais réserver un vol de retour plus tôt. Votre pays a sucé tout le bonheur hors de moi.

★ No thank you. I don't want extra fries with my fries.
   Non merci. Je ne veux pas frites supplémentaire avec mes frites.

★ No. I don't want to discuss the Treaty of Lisbon or the Central Bank.
   Non, je ne veux pas discuter le traité de Lisbonne ou la Banque centrale.

Five reasons you know you're in Belgium

❶ **Belgians love their beer** 'A Belgian goes into a bar' is not a joke. It's a perpetual occurrence.

❷ **The country is flat and featureless, like its population** Don't expect any degree of excitement from either.

❸ **Locals confuse 'picturesque' with 'lacklustre.'** Similarly, they confuse the phrase 'hidden gem' with 'nothing to do here.'

④ **You're perpetually wet. And when you're not wet, you're damp.** Belgium enjoys an average of 200 days of rain per year, which means it's either raining, about to rain, or has just finished raining.

⑤ **You'll get French fries served with absolutely everything** The Belgians claim they invented French fries and take every opportunity to ram this fact – and the food – down your throat. There's even a whole museum dedicated to French fries in Bruges (see above.)

WHAT'S WRONG WITH
EUROPEAN BUDGET AIRLINES?

IN A WORD, 'everything'. In two words, 'lying bastards'. A concept that must have been inspired by Machiavelli himself, low cost European airlines confuse the phrase 'revolutionising short-haul flight' with the concept of 'colossal levels of deception'.

The dishonesty begins when you discover that the airport you arrive at shares the name of your destination city but not its actual geographic location. For example: If, for any reason, you ever find yourself needing to take a budget airline to Barcelona, it would be reasonable to expect to land within a 20–30-minute bus or cab ride from Barcelona, and not on the outskirts of Madrid. Or Marseilles.

But that's just one of the many delights of European budget airlines …

What European budget airlines say	What they actually mean
No frills	A level of service that would embarrass even a white-goods superstore or your local council
Ample leg room	If you're Oscar Pistorius
Low fares	Before you take into account eye-watering extra charges for printing your boarding pass at the airport, any checked-in luggage, speedy boarding, guaranteed seat allocation and anything else we can screw out of you

What European budget airlines say	What they actually mean
Safety is our number one concern	Profitability is our number one concern
Travel insurance is entirely optional	We'll use every scare tactic at our disposal to convince you to buy this from us at inflated prices; and anyway, you probably won't even realise it's added automatically at the payment stage and you have to 'uncheck' the tiny hidden box if you don't actually want it
No credit card fees apply	Credit card fees still apply … we've just renamed them 'administration fees'
Free carry-on baggage allowance	Providing your carry-on luggage is no bigger than a bum bag or a large packet of crisps
Low levels of flight delays and rescheduling	Compared to Air Congo and Kazakhstan Airways
You can easily amend your details after booking	As long as you're happy to pay extortionate charges for the privilege
Wide selection of reasonably priced in-flight refreshments	Assuming you find hotel mini-bar prices 'reasonable'
No hidden charges	Hidden charges

BULGARIA

So what if you misplaced a little weapons-grade uranium?
The important thing is keeping track of all those
handmade doileys and goat hair rugs.
Conan O'Brien

CHEAP WINE WITH the taste and consistency of cough syrup, budget ski holidays and umbrella-wielding Cold War assassins. Bulgaria is all this and more. Unfortunately the 'more' includes concrete tower blocks that redefine the words brutal and repugnant, widespread corruption and dangerous levels of air pollution. Despite the country's first free elections taking place in 1990, these are all constant reminders that Bulgaria was once an industrialised Stalinist state.

Other legacies from over forty-five years of Soviet rule include queuing and form-filling. The idea of a paperless society is anathema to Bulgarian officialdom. Forms have to be completed for everything. Sometimes you need to fill out a form just to be able to fill out a different form.

It's been difficult for Bulgaria to make the transition to a free market economy and the country suffers from one of the lowest standards of living in the EU. It's not surprising then to learn that Bulgaria is also the European country that ranks the lowest in the World Happiness Report. This is particularly evident in Bulgarians working in the hospitality industry for whom the term 'service with a smile' is incomprehensible, there being no understanding of the words 'service' or 'smile'.

CHALGA: BULGARIA'S VERSION OF HIP-HOP

Combining modern dance beats with traditional Balkan and gypsy folk music rhythms, Chalga is a huge cultural phenomenon in Bulgaria. Go to any town or city and the hordes of young people lining the street are likely to be queuing not for bread (as you might think), but to get in to Chalga Clubs.

Although its popularity shows no signs of abating, this music scene is controversial; its critics claim it corrupts the youth, promoting a luxurious lifestyle that's beyond the reach of most of the population. With lyrics glamorising easy money, crime, aggression and promiscuous women, Chalga has been described as the Bulgarian version of the hip-hop scene … but the two are easy to tell apart.

3 ways to tell the difference between rap music and Chalga music:

Names
- Rap artists are called: L'il Wayne, Jay Z, Notorious B.I.G
- Chalga artists are called: MC Lanevski, Gangsta Yamorov, Mixmasta Atanasoff

Song topics
- Rap artists sing about: glocks, hoes, the hood, homies, money, bling and cops
- Chalga artists sing about: stray dogs, bureaucracy and root vegetables

Clothing
- Rap artists wear: a bandana half covered by a baseball cap; a brightly coloured basketball shirt; extra baggy jeans and Nike Hi Tops
- Chalga artists wear: gypsy blouses, colourful waistcoats, baggy trousers and sandals.

SOFIA

Despite being one of Europe's oldest capital cities with a history that stretches over seven millennia, Sofia will always be a disappointment to visitors, having absolutely no 'must-see' attractions. However, what Sofia lacks in famous landmarks, it more than makes up for in stray dogs; up to 10,000 wander the city, many travelling in packs.

Did you know?

Byala Slatina, Stara Zagora, and Gorna Oryahovitsa are not three deadly female Russian assassins who feature in Bond films. They are actual names of Bulgarian cities.

Attractions to avoid

★ **Alexander Nevski Church** 'The most imposing church in Sofia' is not a huge come-on. However, arrive here with low expectations and you will not be disappointed. Only worth a visit if you like gloomy interiors, being pestered by beggars as soon as you arrive and being pestered by a different set of beggars as soon as you leave.

★ **The Rotunda of St George** The oldest building in Sofia (and that's the most interesting thing about it).

★ **Vitosha Mountain** Sofia might claim this is its greatest attraction but it's lying. This mountain lies outside the city to the south and is promoted as a ski resort, albeit a ski resort that lacks any sort of infrastructure. The film *Rage of the Yeti* was filmed here in 2010; after experiencing slow lifts, inadequate car parking and a lack of acceptable dining facilities it's not surprising the yeti was unhappy.

★ **Varna: the last resort** The holiday resort of Varna is known within Bulgaria as the 'playground of the rich'. However, it's important to point out that this description is relative in a country where, for many people, instant coffee and shoes are considered luxury goods.

The local tourist authority promotes the fact that Varna lies on the same latitude as Biarritz in France, yet that's where any similarity ends. The reality is that this Black Sea seaside resort is the Bulgarian equivalent of Blackpool, offering the same level of charm and sophistication.

Varna itself features a dolphinarium that's been described as 'depressing and upsetting' and the Bonkers Disco, where the name is inversely proportionate to the amount of fun you'll experience. There are a number of different beach resorts within Varna itself, offering attractions like water parks as short on rides as they are thrills and diving schools which seem to have difficulty comprehending the terms 'qualified instructors' and 'safety'.

The well-known Golden Sands resort in Varna features a 1:10 scale replica of the Eiffel Tower but no one knows why and even fewer care.

FIVE ABSOLUTELY TRUE FACTS ABOUT BULGARIA
(NONE OF WHICH WILL INSPIRE YOU TO VISIT)

★ Bagpipes are used in traditional Bulgarian folk music.
★ Bulgaria is known as the 'homeland of yogurt'.
★ Sofia is foggy for an average of thirty-three days per year.
★ If you don't speak Bulgarian you can get by with Russian.
★ Bulgarians were the first people to use the Cyrillic alphabet after its inception in the ninth century.

Five reasons you know you're in Bulgaria

1 You're probably lost Many of the road signs are in the Cyrillic alphabet only. Due to the high number of tourists who get lost and run out of fuel in remote mountain passes, authorities recommend packing a good map, a compass, a bountiful supply of food and bedding, and a flare pistol.

❷ **You're probably coughing** There's no legal minimum age for smoking in Bulgaria and many children start smoking at about seven, becoming regular smokers by twelve.

❸ **You're probably dead** Apart from packs of rabid dogs in towns and cities, the countryside is also home to brown bears, wolves and two types of venomous snakes, all of which have been known to attack humans.

❹ **You're probably in a queue** Queuing is as much a way of life in Bulgaria as ugly architecture; but be warned, these are unruly, ill-disciplined queues. There's a saying that a Bulgarian would climb inside your asshole just to get a few inches closer to the front of the line.

❺ **It's easy to get into a fight, or at least an argument with the locals** In Bulgarian culture a nod of the head actually means 'no' and shaking the head from side to side means 'yes'. This can have both comical and tragic results.

USEFUL BULGARIAN PHRASES

★ For god's sake, smile!
   За Бога, усмихнете се!
★ I don't smoke. Please don't spit at me and look upon me as a social leper or an extraterrestrial.
   Не пуша. Моля не плюй по мен и гледай на мен като социален прокажен или извънземно.
★ Can you help me? I have immediate need of a rabies shot.
   Може ли да ми помогнете? Имам непосредствена нужда от бяс изстрел.

CROATIA

A bloody and brutal four-year war of independence... for this?
Anonymous

FOR TEN YEARS Croatia has waited patiently behind the rope at the EU headquarters in Brussels being told, 'If your name's not on the list, you're not coming in.' Desperate pleas of 'Do you know who I am?' were answered with 'Yes. An impoverished Balkan state with a reputation for state corruption, uncontrolled organised crime and a shameful human rights record.' Eventually it managed to blag its way in and on 1 July 2013 Croatia became the twenty-eighth country suckered into joining the European Union.

Since winning its independence from the former Yugoslavia in a lengthy and violent war, Croatia has a clear new political identity but has struggled to find its real character. Once best known only to map makers and CNN journalists, Croatia has been searching for a long, long time for the right way to position itself on the world stage. The following are authentic, but often ill-considered, ways that Croatia has attempted to promote itself to appeal to international visitors:

'The Mediterranean as it once was': Croatians should take another look at their atlas. Their country is actually located on the Adriatic.

'The country of olive oil': No it isn't. You're confusing yourself with Spain, Italy or Greece.

'Europe's most fashionable hotspot': This might be true in the same way that puffball skirts, lace fingerless gloves and fluorescent shell-suits were once considered fashionable.

'The Golden Breadbasket of Europe': WTF!

A country best known for two things, war and inventing the neck tie, Croatia vies with Malta as a destination to visit only if every other Southern European resort is fully booked. What it lacks in style and sophistication it more than makes up in uncomfortably hot summer temperatures, overcrowding and an overwhelming bitter hatred towards the Serbs.

The tourist authority has recently taken to claiming that Croatia is currently Europe's 'it' destination. They forgot to add the 's' and the 'h'.

THE NECK TIE: CROATIA'S GREATEST INVENTION

Gunpowder, the printing press, the steam locomotive, the internal combustion engine, penicillin... some countries have their names writ large in the book of the world's greatest ever inventions and discoveries. Croatia is not one of them. It will be best remembered for inventing the neck tie which owes its origins to the decorative cravats worn by Croatian soldiers fighting in the European Thirty Year War (1618-48). Croatia calls this invention 'a global cultural contribution.'

They are so wrong.

ZAGREB

The capital, located in the north of the country, is often described as a 'happening city' or a 'city coming into its own as a destination'; these are just euphemisms for somewhere so dull that no one can think of anything positive to say about it. Remember: a glut of Austro-Hungarian architecture and a daily vegetable market are never adequate reasons to visit a city.

CROATIA: IT'S A MINEFIELD!

Quite literally...

During the war for independence up to 2 million mines were laid in Croatian inland areas. In the fog of war these were laid haphazardly and no accurate records remain of their location. Authorities think that there are 250,000 mines that still remain unexploded. Thankfully, however, since 2009, all known minefields are now marked. You can identify these locations by the international symbol of an inverted red triangle containing a skull and crossbones. That or by the presence of littered lower body parts.

Attractions to avoid

★ **The Museum of Broken Relationships** Yes, this is a real museum where members of the public have donated personal effects left over from former lovers, accompanied by a brief description of the doomed relationship. Most of the stories are exceedingly depressing and it is recommended only for those who delight in schadenfreude.

★ **Croatian Museum of Naive Art** Another comical-sounding but authentic attraction, this time featuring works characterised by what critics call 'childlike simplicity'. Be prepared for erroneous perspectives, unsubtle colours and finding yourself over-using the phrase, 'You're having a laugh'.

★ **Botanical Gardens** A chance to experience what Kew Gardens would be like if it didn't have any funding and was run by people who don't care.

DUBROVNIK

Located in the far south of the country on the Adriatic Sea, Dubrovnik is often described as '*the* place in Croatia for celebrity spotting'. Although this is accurate, foreign visitors are advised to prepare for disappointment as the celebrities spotted will most likely include basketball player Peja Stojakovic, talk show host Sanja Dolezal and film director Vinko Bresan.

Although heavily shelled by the Serbian army, the locals are proud that no marauding forces ever successfully breached the massive city walls; that presupposes, however, that there was any reason to enter Dubrovnik in the first place.

The city was described by George Bernard Shaw as 'Paradise on earth', but then again, he didn't get out much.

FIVE ABSOLUTELY TRUE FACTS ABOUT CROATIA
(NONE OF WHICH WILL INSPIRE YOU TO VISIT)

★ Apart from the neck tie (see separate panel), Croatia is immensely proud that it invented the principle of Double Entry Book Keeping.
★ Croatia ranks 42nd in the world for the purity of its water
★ In 2009 it held the record for producing the world's longest sausage (1,738 feet)
★ Many guidebooks point out that friendly, attentive service should be a pleasant surprise rather than an expectation
★ Croatia's real name is 'Hrvatska'; not so much the name of a country as a Countdown letter selection

---

Attractions to avoid

★ **Ancient city walls** Visitors can walk a mile around the old city on top of its ancient fortified walls, some of which are 82 feet high in places. Not recommended for those scared of the following: heights, extortionate ticket prices, a lack of toilets or slipping to their death.
★ **The Old Town** Dominated by restaurants and cafes, the Old Town mainly exists to serve the needs of the 6,000 tourists dumped here each day at lunchtime by the countless cruise ships arriving in

Dubrovnik Port. Following their tour guides through the narrow streets like cattle, these visitors are viewed appropriately by the locals as cash-cows and since they're day-trippers who won't be returning, restauranteurs have absolutely no need to make an effort. Worth visiting if you want to experience some of the very worst and most overpriced food in Croatia.

★ **Dubrovnik cable car** Although described by some as 'unstable and scary', the cable car provides good views over the city providing you're standing next to a window and not stuck in the middle of the often overcrowded and sweltering cabin. Many visitors are put off by the long wait between rides (it only runs every thirty minutes) and because they want to live to talk about their holiday.

DID YOU KNOW?

★ The Croatian word for hello is 'bog!'
★ The Croatian currency is named after a small rodent belonging to the weasel family, the Kuna. This consists of 100 Lipas.
★ Proud Croatia claims that electricity pioneer and inventor Nikola Tesla who invented AC current was Croatian. He wasn't, he was Serbian (as he declared himself).

Other places to avoid

★ **Split** The largest Croatian city on the Adriatic coast and possibly the dreariest. So named because you'll want to leave as soon as you arrive.
★ **The Adriatic coastline** The way the Croatians go on and on and on about the almost 2,000 miles of coastline would make you think theirs was the only country in the world with beaches. The tourist office

incessantly promotes the fact that Croatia's coastal areas are completely undeveloped. However, this is not due to a desire to retain their natural, unspoiled characteristics, but more the consequence of a country too broke to do anything about it.

★ **The Frog Museum, Lokve** This real museum, 80 miles south west of Zagreb, features exhibits documenting 1,000 species of frogs from around the world including a remarkable collection of frog sound recordings. The organisers claim a visit here is an 'unforgettable, thought-provoking and exciting experience' with a complete lack of irony.

USEFUL CROATIAN PHRASES

★ I am sorry for calling your country the former Yugoslavia. I didn't realise you were so touchy about it.
Žao mi je što ste zvali vaša zemlja bivše Jugoslavije. Nisam znao da si tako osjetljiva o tome.

★ I don't want to complain, but a pavement café and an amusement arcade that remain open until 10.30 p.m. do not constitute what I understand to be 'dynamic nightlife'.
Ne želim se žaliti, ali kolnika kafić i zabavni arkada koje ostaje otvorena do 22.30 ne čine ono što ja razumijem da se 'dinamičan noćni život.'

★ Venison goulash and prunes is your country's signature dish. Really?
Gulaš od divljači i šljive je vaše zemlje potpis jelo. Stvarno?

Five reasons you know you're in Croatia

① **You're probably hungry** Croatian cuisine is influenced by the culinary styles of Hungary, Turkey, Slovenia and Austria. In this context the terms 'cuisine' and 'culinary style' are used in the very loosest sense.

❷ **Every single person talks about Goran Ivanisevic** As the only internationally famous living Croatian, locals don't miss any opportunity – however tenuous – to drop his name into conversation e.g.

You: That's a nice dog.

Croatian: Thanks. He likes chasing tennis balls. Did you know that Goran Ivanisevic is the only wild card player to win the men's singles at Wimbledon.

❸ **Hospitality can change into hostility at a moment's notice** One moment you might be drinking beer with the locals in a Zagreb bar; the next you might be getting hit in the face with a broken glass. All it takes is to casually mention something like the fact that Serbians are the most welcoming and open people you've ever met or that Belgrade was simply charming. Not only should you not mention the war … for your own personal safety you should also not mention any of the states of the former Yugoslavia. Particularly Serbia.

❹ **Music festivals are omnipresent** Croatia is trying to position itself as a viable alternative to Ibiza for people who don't want the crowds or the cost – or, after looking at the various line-ups, the top artists. At the time of writing acts scheduled for this year's festivals include: Kollektiv Turmstrasse, Bicep, Shonky, Christopher Rau, Kode 9 and Bonobo. Also on the bill is someone called John Roberts who the promoters say is one of electronic music's top innovators. However, with a name like that, he is more likely to be a carpet fitter.

❺ **You'll be even more exasperated and irritated in July and August** Not only is this time of year stinking hot (literally), you'll find Croatia's fragile infrastructure battling to cope with the overwhelming influx of tourists. Everything is more crowded, more expensive, more irritating – and more shouty – since most of the holidaymakers are Italians and Germans.

EUROPEAN CUISINE: NOT SO MUCH FOOD, AS A WAY OF USING WASTE ANIMAL PARTS

BRITISH FOOD MIGHT not be the most exciting or ambitious but at least a) you know roughly what you're getting and b) it's usually edible. In Europe it's a whole different story.

Europeans call their cooking 'cuisine' to make their dishes sound interesting and glamorous but in reality this is just an excuse to eat parts of animals that even the Chinese would frown upon. Beware of meals whose exotic-sounding names hide culinary abominations. For example, order *nozki* in Poland and you'll be served a plate of jellied pig trotters, select *kiaulės ausis* in Lithuania and you'll be able to tuck in to a selection of smoked pig's ears or go for the delicacy *stracotto d'asino* in northern Italy and you'll end up with a bowl of donkey stew.

Supporters of continental cuisine point out just how creative and inventive European chefs have been over the centuries. This, of course, is correct. After all, who else would have had the imagination to think that cooking offal with two other types of offal was a good idea?

Real European foods to avoid at all costs

★ **BEUSCHEL:** This traditional dish from Vienna is better known as lung stew and is usually made with veal lungs and heart. With a recipe that usually begins 'separate the veal lung from the windpipe and gullet', is there any need to say more?

★ **CASU MARZU:** This Sardinian dish consists of sheep's milk cheese containing live maggots to help break down the cheese fats, soften it and imbue it with an unique flavour. The insect larvae are eaten with the cheese. Not so much a food as a biological weapon.

★ **BEEF TATARE:** Popular in Austria, Belgium, France, Denmark and Germany it's difficult to know what's most repellent about this dish: the fact it consists of a patty of raw beef or horse meat, or the fact it's often garnished with a raw egg. If you think you have a high resistance towards E. coli, Salmonella or vomiting, then this is the dish for you.

★ **VÉRES HURKA:** A Hungarian sausage usually made by boiling pig or cattle blood until it's congealed and then adding boiled and minced pig's organs and rice. Formerly looked upon as a meal of the poor, the dish should nowadays be looked upon as a meal for the desperate.

★ **HORSE MEAT:** Compared to some of the abominations served across the continent, eating horse meat seems positively normal, which is why it appears in sausages, stews, steaks and hamburgers in most European countries (and also some mislabelled ready meals in the UK). Horse meat can be found in most French supermarkets alongside pink veal, but then that probably doesn't surprise you.

★ **LUTEFISK:** It's often wise to avoid food described as being 'gelatinous in texture' or having a 'pungent, offensive odour'. Lutfisk, an aged whitefish that's popular in Denmark, Finland and Sweden, has both these qualities and if that wasn't bad enough, has often been described as being 'infamously unpleasant'. Those experiencing the Lutefisk aroma for the first time have compared the sensation as like 'being hit with CS gas'.

★ **HEAD CHEESE:** Nothing to do with cheese but everything to do with skinning the head of a sheep, pig or cow then boiling it until the flesh is tender and falls off the bone. The collagen in the bone marrow makes the whole mixture congeal into solidified gelatine, which is then sliced and left to cool down, then served on salad or in a sandwich. Popular in many European countries, think of it as a sort of primordial spam – but even less appealing.

★ **ROOSTER TESTICLE SOUP:** There's absolutely no excuse for not knowing what you're letting yourself in for when you see this dish on a Hungarian menu. The testicles have been described as tasting like tofu. However, this comparison alone should be enough to put you off.

★ **BLOOD EGGS:** Just what it is with the Hungarians and appalling food? Another of their traditional dishes, this one involves cooking scrambled eggs in pig's blood – traditionally, blood from the first pig killed that season. The pig is considered more fortunate than those having to eat the actual meal.

★ **CRIADILLAS:** You might see this dish on a Spanish menu under its more innocuous name, 'bull fries'. Some Spaniards think that eating the testicles of prized bulls makes you brave and more masculine. In reality it just makes you unsettled and more nauseous.

★ **POLŠJA OBARA:** There aren't many dormice in Slovenia. Not because of efficient pest control or deforestation, but because the locals find them so damned tasty. This is a thick soup or stew made of potatoes, spices, apple vinegar and, of course, dormice. (NB This dish is completely unrelated to ratatouille.)

★ **COCKSCOMB:** Not what you probably think it is, but still just as loathsome. Cockscombs are the floppy red fleshy things on top of roosters' heads that look like weird upside-down gloves. Why anyone would have a) ever wondered what they tasted like and b) decided they should be an important component of many Italian dishes and sauces defies stupidity.

★ **LAPPKOK:** Served in Sweden and Finland, the genius who came up with the idea of making dumplings (called blodpalt) from reindeer blood mixed with wheat or rye flour probably wondered if it was still possible to make this dish any more abhorrent. The answer was a resounding 'yes', which is why it's traditionally served with reindeer bone marrow.

★ **TÊTE DE VEAU:** Revered as a delicacy in France and also popular in Germany, Belgium and Italy, this dish is made by boiling the flesh of a calf's head, then serving it in a gelatinous broth with calf's brain on the top or cutting it into squares and serving it accompanied by side orders of assorted offal including calf kidneys, pancreas and testicles. As they say in France, 'rien ne se perd, tout se tranforme' (waste not, want not.)

CYPRUS

> Realizing that they will never be a world power, the Cypriots
> have decided to be a world nuisance.
>
> *George Mikes*

IF COUNTRIES WERE Robert Louis Stevenson novels* then Cyprus would be less *Treasure Island* and more *Dr Jekyll and Mr Hyde*.

On one hand the tiny island, inhabited since 10,000 BC, is known as the birthplace of Aphrodite and the 'crossroads of civilisation'.

On the other hand, thanks to a €10 billion EU bailout and vicious levels of taxation, Cyprus is just about keeping its head above water, providing a package holiday destination for tourists with low budgets and even lower expectations. Think of it as an Essex suburb that's been lifted up wholesale and dumped back down again in the eastern Mediterranean.

The result is that Cyprus is a place where Roman mosaics, Byzantine churches and early Christian basilicas sit side by side with The Queen Vic karaoke bar, Nelson's Nightclub and Molly Malone's Irish pub. And like Dr Jekyll and Mr Hyde, it's the morally reprehensible personality that's the dominant one. Although it *is* possible to walk in the footsteps of ancient empires, most visitors find themselves traipsing behind shrieking hen parties from Basildon or a bunch of drunken Romford plumbers.

It's true. Cyprus is at a crossroads – but it's not of civilisation … it's at the intersection of Chav Street and Pikey Avenue.

*And they're not, by the way.

Attractions to avoid

★ **St. Nicholas of the Cats (edge of Akrotiri village, Limassol)** Legend has it that in the fourth century this area was overrun with poisonous snakes, making it impossible to build the monastery. The solution was to bring in hundreds of cats to kill them with the result that the creatures stayed and formed a colony that exists today. This is an interesting place to visit if you want to see old nuns and malnourished cats.

★ **Owl and Byzantine Iconography Museum (Larnaca)** *The* place to visit if you are culturally fulfilled by the sight of ancient Byzantine scripts and over 5,700 ornaments and pictures of owls.

★ **Ocean Aquarium (between Paralimni and Protara)** It would be difficult to imagine a sadder collection of marine life. Worth a visit if you want to see small tanks, neglected pens and dirty water – and a small selection of depressed-looking fish, miserable penguins, suicidal turtles and gloomy crocodiles. Not so much an aquarium as a prime target for animal rights protestors.

CYPRUS FIGHT CLUB

Cyprus has a long history of fighting. The Mycenaeans, Byzantines, Egyptians, Assyrians, Persians, Romans, Venetians and Ottomans – and more recently, Turkey and Greece – all fought bloody battles over the island. It's a practice that continues today. Go into any resort bar on a Saturday night and you'll find British holidaymakers in replica football shirts keeping this historic tradition alive.

Ayia Napa

Although Cyprus is known as the birthplace of Aphrodite, a visit to Ayia Napa (literally, 'Streets That Flow With Vomit') will convince you that Dionysus, the god of drunkenness and debauchery, was not only also born there, but is still very much in residence. Once a small fishing village, Ayia Napa was developed to cater for a specific type of holidaymaker: those who like gambling on whether their drinks are laced with Rohypnol, who want to sleep in sick-encrusted clothes on the beach or who prefer to indulge in dalliances with bar staff infested with crabs.

Five reasons you know you're in Cyprus

❶ **A recent sudden influx of foreign visitors** Unfortunately for the local economy these are not hordes of holidaymakers but journalists, analysts and assorted ne'er sayers arriving at Nicosia Airport to report on the island's interminable slide into financial oblivion.

❷ **There's a shortage of magic markers and thick felt pens** Protesting locals have bought these up in their hundreds so they can draw Hitler moustaches on pictures of Angela Merkel.

❸ **... and Prozac** How else do you think the locals can deal with day-to-day life?

❹ **Signs outside shops that say, 'We accept hummus'** There are those who are already looking for a currency with more long-term stability than the euro.

❺ **An air of despondency and gloom that sticks to the Island like the smell of rancid halloumi** The general feeling of pessimism is not helped by news stories like the recent report on the world's strongest economies: Cyprus came out at number 214; there are only 196 countries.

Did you know?

- On the face it, a 'Cypriot cabaret' is somewhere you might expect to see a Bucks Fizz tribute act, a bad ventriloquist or a third-rate magician called Mr Mysterio. The reality is somewhat different; these places are actually brothels associated with organised crime.
- Cypriot Cock Drops is not a medication for Gonorrhoea; it's actually the revoltingly named local equivalent of Angostura bitters.

A country of two halves ...

The reasons why Turkey invaded northern Cyprus in 1974 are far too complicated and boring to go into here. All you need to know is that they involved a military coup in Greece, a desire to protect the interests of Turkish Cypriots and lamb kleftiko. The result is a divided island. The Turks control the northern part and the Greeks control the south. 'Greek Cyprus' is best for all-day English breakfasts, catching Chlamydia, having your wallet stolen and drinking from goldfish bowls filled to the brim with brandy and lemon juice. The north is best for political propaganda, power cuts, nesting turtles and knife fights.

Five absolutely true facts about Cyprus
(none of which will inspire you to visit)

- Cyprus is one of the largest manufacturers of cement.
- Public transport can be best described as either 'inadequate' or 'non-existent'.
- The Weever fish buries itself in the sand in Cypriot costal waters. Treading on it results in painful stinging which can cause seizures, gangrene and, in some cases, death.
- The two most famous Cypriot music artists are Peter André and Tulisa.
- Summers here can last for eight months. So can ennui.

USEFUL CYPRIOT PHRASES

★ Does the sign 'Closed for business' refer to this shop or the entire country?

Εμφανίζεται η ένδειξη «Κλειστό για επαγγελματικούς λόγους», αναφέρονται σε αυτό το κατάστημα ή το σύνολο της χώρας;

★ Yes, I have €200 in my wallet but that's no reason to carry me shoulder high through the streets!

Ναι, έχω € 200 στο πορτοφόλι μου, αλλά αυτός δεν είναι λόγος για να με μεταφέρουν ώμο υψηλή στους δρόμους!

★ As far as Germany's century-old quest to take over Europe goes, it looks as though it might be third time lucky.

Όσον αφορά αιωνόβια αναζήτηση της Γερμανίας να αναλάβει η Ευρώπη πηγαίνει, φαίνεται σαν να μπορεί να είναι η τρίτη φορά τυχερός.

THE CZECH REPUBLIC

A land of disappointments.
Anonymous

RUDYARD KIPLING ONCE wrote, 'East is East, and West is West, and never the twain shall meet.'

The Czech Republic violently disagrees with his assumption and points out that due to its central location in Europe, not only is it the very nation where East *does* meet West,* it's this geographic providence that enables the Czech Republic to offer visitors the 'very best of both worlds'.

Don't be fooled though. Just as there are no 'best parts' of being kicked in the balls, there are no 'best parts' of Eastern Europe. Visit the Czech Republic and you'll find a relatively modern country with a reasonable infrastructure and growing economy; but underneath this thin veneer of familiarity you'll see a country where life reads like a Franz Kafka novel – a place full of existential despair where ordinary people are overpowered by brutal bureaucracy, making them feel disorientated, perplexed and helpless.

However, for 'ordinary people', read 'tourists'.

It's said that no matter where your travels take you in Europe, you're bound to pass through the Czech Republic at some point. If this is the case, then you should seriously consider re-planning your route so that 'pass through' becomes 'circumnavigate'.

* This can also be interpreted as a place where low standards meet high expectations.

PRAGUE

The Steve Martin of capital cities, Prague is seriously overrated and relies on a massive amount of goodwill and history for its appeal. Czechs themselves describe the city as offering a 'melange of glorious architecture'. The word 'melange' is used on purpose to make the city sound more cosmopolitan than it is and also because by the time you look it up to see what it means, you've forgotten any objections you might have had to visiting Prague in the first place.

DID YOU KNOW?

Many horror films have been shot in the Czech Republic including *Hostel*, *From Hell*, *Howling II*, *The Golem* and the remake of *The Omen*. *Mission Impossible* was also filmed here and, while not a horror film, the title is reflective of someone attempting to have a good time on holiday.

Attractions to avoid

★ **Horse carriage tour** What you want is a romantic journey through Old Prague, the rhythm of horses' hooves echoing across the ancient city's cobblestones … What you get is a jerky bone-shaking ride, the all-pervasive, pungent stench of horse urine and a surly driver who cares as much about you as he does for his animals.

★ **The Charles Bridge** Crossing the Vltava River on this fourteenth-century bridge is easier than it sounds. The reality is that you have to force your way past hordes of tourists, souvenir sellers, food vendors, beggars, artists and itinerant musicians that block your path every inch of the way. An unsatisfying experience for anyone other than pickpockets.

★ **Petrin Hill: Eiffel Tower replica** Visiting this 197-foot replica of the Eiffel Tower enables you to experience overpriced admission, bad service, rude staff and disappointing views without having to set foot in Paris.

★ **Everywhere** The Czech Republic is absolutely brimming with thousands of ancient ornate castles and a colourful, rich and romantic past replete with good kings, evil counts, the Knights Templar, heroic wars, courageous victories and good rising up against evil. The Czech Republic might have a fairytale history but long queues, confusing ticketing arrangements, expensive admissions, scowling officious staff, poor audio guides, inaccurate information and random closures without warning mean it's doubtful your excursions will have a happy ending.

FIVE ABSOLUTELY TRUE FACTS ABOUT THE CZECH REPUBLIC
(NONE OF WHICH WILL INSPIRE YOU TO VISIT*)

★ It has one of the highest densities of castles in the world.
★ The country's best-known invention is Semtex plastic explosive.
★ It's home to the largest shoe manufacturer in the world.
★ The Czech have their own, slightly less appealing, version of Nutella; Skvarkova Pomazanka is a popular pork fat spread that also contains crunchy fried meat chunks.
★ The Czech Republic Tourist Agency lists the three most compelling reasons to visit the country as an abundance of castle ruins, underground caves and formal gardens.

*Unless you want to buy Semtex. Or shoes.

Five reasons you know you're in the Czech Republic

❶ **Footwear that would give Jimmy Choo apoplexy** Fashion and footwear are as far apart in the Czech Republic as the country's Romany beggars and their respect for property. Sandals worn with long socks are as much a part of the national psyche as form-filling, police brutality and dumplings.

❷ **1984-levels of bureaucracy** It won't surprise you to learn that a few years ago, completely without irony, the Czech government set up a special commission with two sub committees and four steering groups to investigate the problem of red tape.

❸ **Easter high jinks** On Easter Monday there's a tradition of men pouring buckets of water over unmarried women and whipping them with thin birch or willow branch. And they say romance is dead.

❹ **Old people with miserable, staring eyes** They're everywhere. In the street and shops. On the trains, trams and buses. Their expression is one of resentment, jealously, bitterness and unbridled hatred. You'll find that most of them work in the hospitality and service industries.

❺ **Food to die from, not for** An abundance of red meat, saturated fats, potatoes, dumplings and salt makes demands on the human digestive system (and general well-being) not seen since woolly mammoths were hunted and eaten raw.

Useful Czech phrases

★ Hello mister policeman. Please stop beating me up for no reason.
Dobrý den pane policista. Prosím, přestalo bít mě bez důvodu.

★ Do you have anything else on the menu except dumplings and sauerkraut?
Vai jums ir kaut kas cits uz izvēlnes izņemot klimpām un kāpostus?

★ I would rather eat my foot that visit yet another set of castle ruins.
Raději bych jíst nohu, že návštěva ještě jeden soubor zříceninu hradu.

DENMARK

Beer is the Danish national drink and the Danish
national weakness is another beer.
Clementine Paddleford

THERE ARE LIES, damn lies and contentment surveys. If you read the results of those studies that are routinely published every couple' of years you'd believe that Denmark is one of the happiest nations on earth, offering one of the best qualities of life.

But visit the country and you'd see a very different picture, a picture painted by the current fashionable Nordic noir crime thrillers set there like *The Killing* and *The Bridge*, or even *Borgen*. This genre depicts Denmark as a sombre, conservative country with rain-swept, windy landscapes and a population that's solemn, reserved, defensive and quite insular. This is one case where TV doesn't lie.

Danish Vikings were among the first to realise they were living in such a lacklustre, soulless, godforsaken country and used exploration and conquest as an excuse to travel down the French coast, around Portugal and Spain into the Mediterranean and as far as modern Istanbul just to find somewhere better (and if they decided that Istanbul was more appealing, just imagine what Denmark was like.)

If you think of Scandinavia as one big happy family, then Denmark is the poor relation. Being geographically separate from Norway, Sweden and Finland has meant it had to develop its own style and culture.

Unfortunately this has involved chairs, fairy tales, miniature plastic bricks and weak lager.

Shakespeare said that something is rotten in the state of Denmark. He was talking about the people and the places.

FIVE ABSOLUTELY TRUE FACTS ABOUT DENMARK
(NONE OF WHICH WILL INSPIRE YOU TO VISIT)

★ Danish shops offer the double-whammy. High prices and a 25% sales tax.
★ Denmark has the world's biggest sperm bank.
★ Sex with animals is not illegal.
★ There are more pigs than people (see above).
★ There is no word for 'please' in the Danish vocabulary.

COPENHAGEN

Capital cities should be dynamic, vibrant, buzzing ... even second-rate ones are usually described as 'lively'. The official Danish Tourist Board website describes Copenhagen as 'the world's cosiest capital city'; this is not an endearing description of its warmth or sense of community, but a damning indictment of its provincial attitude.

In the film *Hans Christian Andersen*, Danny Kaye sang, 'Wonderful, Wonderful Copenhagen'. He was lying.

Attractions to avoid

★ **The Little Mermaid** If you plan to visit this statue there's a big hint that you're about to be disappointed; it's the world 'Little'. Erected in 1913 to honour Hans Christian Andersen's fairy tale, this 4 ft 1 in. sculpture should be more accurately named the 'The Extremely Unimposing

Mermaid' or the 'Tremendously Underwhelming Mermaid'. To be honest, most statues in the middle of shopping precincts or outside council offices are more imposing. If it was in the middle of the city and you could just stroll past it without much effort you could accept being disillusioned. As it is, you have to make a special trip to the harbour, force your way through coach loads of expectant tourists until you see it set against an ugly industrial backdrop and naval yard. Once voted 'The Most Overrated Tourist Attraction In The World', this statue is easy to find once you're in Copenhagen; just follow the cries of 'Is that it?'

★ **Tivoli Gardens** Described as a 'world-class amusement park', the Tivoli Gardens actually resembles more of a run-down fun fair. The Danish Tourist Authority claim it's 'much more than twenty-nine thrilling and enchanting rides'. They are, of course, correct. It's a place where you can have a near death experience ... and actually wish you'd died.

★ **Nyhavn** Sailors, ale houses and chandlers have been replaced by Japanese tourists, overpriced restaurants and boutiques. Once a busy seventeenth-century commercial port; now a busy twenty-first-century tourist trap.

★ **Carlsberg Brewery Visitor Centre** Probably the biggest waste of time. A dusty ex-brewery that's been transformed into a shiny new gift shop with a visitor centre attached. Here you can enjoy the granary, the old stables, some old brewing vats and the world's largest collection of beer bottles. The price of admission includes two free beers at the brewery bar but the exotic ones you invariably want to taste are often conveniently 'out of stock' and you have to settle for a regular Carlsberg lager you can get at any supermarket.

★ **The Running Tour** The organisers claim the best way to see Copenhagen is by running. No it's not; it's by chauffeured limo (and that's if you even want to go in the first place). The Running Tour involves a guided 90-minute run through the city. If you want to combine sightseeing, pulled hamstrings and debilitating cramp, this is a must.

Useful Danish phrases

★ You may not have come across this before. It's called 'fun'.
Du har måske ikke stødt på dette før. Det hedder "sjov".

★ Why do you consider that politeness and gratitude are signs of superficiality and weakness?
Hvorfor mener du, at høflighed og taknemmelighed er tegn på overfladiskhed og svaghed?

★ I didn't realise that mullets were still fashionable in your country.
Jeg var ikke klar over, at multe var stadig på mode i dit land.

Other places in Denmark to avoid

★ **Christiania** A suburb of Copenhagen, Christiania is synonymous with 'free town' and also 'hypocrisy'. In the 70s, a bunch of hippies turned this former military base into a self-proclaimed independent neighbourhood – and then promptly banned everyone else from moving there. The locals resent visitors and do not allow photography but are happy to sell souvenirs adorned with images of cannabis leaves, Smiley faces or Bob Marley – or all three. Until recently you could also buy actual drugs on Pusher Street (subtle, it isn't).

A sense of lawlessness, poorly maintained buildings, streets strewn with litter and a high proportion of drunks and addicts have made Christiania resemble less of an idyllic commune and more of a shantytown. A more accurate description would be slum.

★ **Legoland** Located in the town of Billund, 150 miles west of Copenhagen, Legoland is the attraction that's as short on interest as the queues are long. It's somewhere that makes Disneyland look good value and the people who run it, benevolent. Here you'll find entry prices that are offensive and refreshment prices that can only be described as obscene. The Eskimos might have twenty words for snow but after visiting here you'll presume the Danes have thirty words for 'rip-off'.

★ **Vikingeskibmuseet (Viking Ship Museum)** Quite frankly, if you've seen one partially restored Viking longboat you've seen them all. Located in Roskilde on the island of Zealand, the museum is described as 'easy to get round', which is a convenient euphemism for 'small without much of interest'.

Five reasons you know you're in Denmark

1. **A quarter of the population share just three surnames** You'll come across a very large number of people called Jensen, Nielsen or Hansen.
2. **There's no obligation to tip restaurant staff** This might sound like a positive thing until you realise it's because you'll rarely receive service that makes you feel like tipping.
3. **Your beer might taste of liquorice** That's because the Danes love liquorice and even put it in their beer (and ice cream).
4. **The proud locals will bore you rigid about how Bluetooth technology was named after their king Harald Bluetooth** It's true. He ate a lot of blueberries ... hence his name.
5. **It's difficult to integrate with the locals** Many visitors get the impression that Danes are unhappy, dour, gloomy – or just plain rude. That's because they are.

EUROTRASH:
THE UNHOLY ALLIANCE OF *MADE IN CHELSEA* AND *THE ONLY WAY IS ESSEX*

SOME PEOPLE CALL them affluent, arrogant, jet-setting, air-kissing hedonists with a penchant for designer labels, gaudy jewellery, plastic surgery and over-bleached hair. Others call them totally self-aware, superficial, degenerate douchebags.

Whatever you think of them (and 'degenerate douchebags' is devastatingly accurate), it's easy to identify whether someone is truly Eurotrash. The first clue is their dress sense. Eurotrash want to look like off-duty models and feel that appropriate daywear is a see-through rib-hugging shirt, leather trousers, fur coat and Uggs. The women dress exactly the same. The second clue is that they are exceptionally shallow. Eurotrash don't just judge a book by its cover, they judge it by the title – except that they don't actually read books, they read *GQ* and *Vogue Italia*.

There are, of course, a number of other clues …

Someone who's Eurotrash ...

★ is decadent, over-cologned and stupid
★ ... and also drug-addicted, pale and sarcastic
★ went to an expensive boarding school somewhere in the Alps and later dropped out of Monaco University
★ spent their teenage years impatiently waiting for their trust fund
★ claims anorexia is a lifestyle choice rather than an eating disorder
★ has swanky apartments in at least three capital cities
★ confuses dressing expensively with dressing badly
★ equates high fashion with wearing something from an endangered species
★ sneers rather than smiles
★ uses the double air-kiss as a default greeting
★ agrees with this statement: 'Eyewear is the lynchpin of the Eurotrash aesthetic.'
★ ... even though they don't know what 'lynchpin' actually means
★ thinks that 160 bpm hardcore techno is the soundtrack to their lives
★ fails to see any irony whatsoever in the character Derek Zoolander

ESTONIA

The world does not understand Estonians, and Estonians
do not understand the world …
Andrei Hvostov

IMAGINE EUROPE AS a large provincial hotel. Then imagine Finland
and the Russian Federation as Championship League footballers in
one of the rooms, having a threesome with a girl of low self-esteem;
that girl is Estonia.

Torn between two lovers, Estonia doesn't know which way to turn. Is
it a Baltic state or a Nordic country? Does it stay loyal to its East
European roots or does it adopt a modern Scandinavian lifestyle. Few
people know and, to be frank, most of the native Estonians don't even
care, having left the country in droves regularly since 1990 (the year
when 10% of the whole population walked out).

This, and its low popularity as a holiday destination, mean that if you
do visit Estonia you won't be caught in queues or traffic jams. That said,
an absence of people is rarely the prime reason to visit a country; if it
were, then the Falklands or Antarctica would be among the top-ten
places to visit.

Estonia is often described as 'Europe's best kept secret'. This is
completely wrong, since anyone knows Europe's best-kept secret is the
barely concealed ambition of Germany to create a United States of
Europe with a single government; metaphorically and physically

trampling with their jack-boots all over the constitutions and sovereignty of individual nation states.

In conclusion, Estonia has very little to offer the locals and even less to offer visitors.

DID YOU KNOW?

★ Although there's just a one-letter difference, it is almost impossible to confuse an Old Estonian with an Old Etonian.

★ An Estonian website claims the country has a strong musical pedigree on the world stage and maintains that the following artists are internationally known and respected: Rudolf Tobias, Arvo Pärt, Veljo Tormis, Lepo Sumera, Erki-Sven Tüür, Kerli, Vaiko Eplik & Ellit and Liris. What part of 'internationally known and respected' don't they understand?

★ An old Estonian proverb is 'Make fun of the man, not of his hat'.

★ Its flag, which consists of equal blue, black and white bands, looks just like a liquorice allsort.

TALLINN

Sounding more like an over-the-counter remedy for cystitis rather than a capital city, Tallinn is famous for offering visitors the chance to be robbed in the picturesque old town surroundings. In this enchanting city, full of old-world charm, you can be pickpocketed while admiring a beautiful fourteenth-century church, have your bag snatched while walking along quaint cobbled streets or be mugged in the shadows of medieval carved stone walls.

Attractions to avoid

★ **Kiek in de Kök** Although its name suggests a painful blow to the groin, this is actually a fifteenth-century watchtower that formed part of the old town's fortifications along with a network of secret tunnels. It now serves as a museum. However, offensive staff with a barely concealed hatred for visitors make a real 'Kiek in de Kök' preferable to the guided tour.

★ **Kalev Marzipan Factory Museum** Even the official website for this attraction makes it sound more like a 'you can't be serious!' rather than a 'must see'. Visit only if you want to learn about the 'colourful history of marzipan'.

★ **NUKU Estonian State Puppet and Youth Theatre** At the time of writing you can watch puppets perform 'A Lollipop and 200 Granddads', 'A Goose Had A Car' and 'Klaabu'. Yes, really. With five stages to watch puppet dramas unfold this venue is perfect if you want to learn about the history of puppetry, attend puppet-making workshops or just want to be somewhere warm for a couple of hours.

★ **Tallinn Zoo** Some critics have called this less a zoo and more the subject of an undercover investigation into poor animal welfare. Visitors should be especially aware of very poor signage and the fact that the Children's Petting Zoo is adjacent to the Siberian tiger enclosure.

ESTONIA AND COMEDY

The legacy of the oppressive Soviet occupation means that Estonia is to stand-up comedy what it is to haute couture. At the time of writing there are no comedy clubs in Estonia and what few jokes do exist, are completely lacking in sophistication or biting satire.

The two current most popular Estonian jokes:

1. Q: How many Russians does it take to change a light bulb?
   A: That's a military secret.

2. 'My dog has no nose.'
   'How does it smell?'
   'It's okay. He has got one really.'

Five reasons you know you're in Estonia

① **You won't see any really old people** Estonia has one of the lowest life expectancy rates in Europe (an average of 72.8 years); the average male life expectancy is 65.

② **But you will see a lot of drunks** The Estonians like their vodka. Very much. Many consider any drink that's less than 20% proof as being 'alcohol free'.

③ **You will never ever, ever, ever be able to understand the locals** This is why: Estonian nouns and adjectives decline in fourteen different cases while the direct object of the verb appears either in the accusative or in the partitive. The accusative coincides with the genitive in the singular and with the nominative in the plural. In addition the Estonian verbal system has no distinctive future tense (the present tense serves here) and features special forms to express an action performed by an undetermined subject. So there.

❹ **Estonians are very wary about tourists** Most of Estonia's history has been one of foreign occupation and domination, which is why the locals are described as 'cautious and reticent'. You'll probably experience this as 'rude and unwelcoming'.

❺ **Levels of environmental pollution that would make members of Greenpeace weep** One of the legacies of the Soviet Army's withdrawal from Estonia in the 1990s was pollution on a level rarely seen outside disaster movies. This included hundreds of thousands of tons of jet fuel dumped into the ground, improperly disposed of toxic chemicals, and discarded outdated explosives and weapons in coastal and inland waters.

USEFUL ESTONIAN PHRASES

✱ After spending just a few days here I can see why your country's most popular export is melancholia.
Pärast kulutuste paar päeva siin ma ei näe põhjust, miks teie riigi populaarseim eksport on melanhoolia.

✱ No thank you. I just want a beer. I do not want a car stolen to order.
Ei, tänan. Ma tahan lihtsalt õlut. Ma ei taha auto varastatud tellida.

✱ I just want to buy a ticket for the museum. Why are you looking at me as if I just spat in your face?
Ma lihtsalt tahan, et osta pilet muuseum. Miks sa vaatad mind, nägu oleksin ma lihtsalt sülitasid oma nägu?

THE EUROVISION SONG CONTEST (BING BING-A-BONG)

T'S DIFFICULT TO know what inspires more hatred: the fact that this insidious event should ever exist or the fact that there seems to be no abating in its popularity. A talent show for the talentless, this is state-funded programming at its very worst; a genre that owes more to a Soviet propaganda film about collectivism than it does to any semblance of modern entertainment.

What began as a cross-border singing contest has slowly putrefied into both a guilty pleasure and a sort of unofficial United Nations General Assembly, albeit one where every sovereign state votes against Britain for a) existing or b) having a world-beating musical legacy that includes the Beatles, punk rock and Cliff Richard.

There's only one thing that justifies the Eurovision Song Contest: instead of laughing at a single contestant, we get the chance to laugh at a whole country.

10 THINGS THE EUROVISION SONG CONTEST
HAS GIVEN THE WORLD — AND WHICH
WE NEITHER NEED NOR WANT

★ Moldovan reggae
★ Armenia's uglier version of Duran Duran
★ Scenes of hideous rampant nationalism that make the Nuremberg rallies look like a Macmillan coffee morning
★ Worthy songs about European unity, peace, harmony or lighting a candle
★ Voting practices that make Russian elections look fair and just
★ Song titles! With lots! Of exclamation marks!
★ Singers with a complete lack of charm, charisma and any ability to hold a tune
★ The balalaika as substitute for an electric guitar
★ Lyrics that include 'schiki micki riki', 'flinga flinga flo' and 'na na na na no'
★ Yet another opportunity for Graham Norton to get on TV

FINLAND

Finland has long been a popular destination with travellers
who enjoy the feeling of knowing that if their car breaks down,
they could be eaten by wolves.
Dave Barry

AS THE LEAST densely populated country in the EU, where lakes and forests account for about 70% of the landmass and where snow covers the country for half of the year, Finland is not so much a country as a wilderness. The Finnish tourist authority promotes the country as somewhere to go to get away from it all; unfortunately the 'all' in this case refers to stimulation, excitement or anything remotely of interest. Other euphemisms are rife. For 'unspoiled and tranquil' read 'dull and boring'. For 'gloriously remote' read 'Don't go'.

In an attempt to create some sort of allure for the country the authorities have also taken to describing Finland as one of Europe's least understood countries ... a land that's 'enigmatic' and 'intriguing.' The biggest mystery, however, must surely be why you'd want to visit in the first place – unless you have more than a passing interest in elks, frozen tundra, mobile phone manufacturing or saunas.

Some countries acknowledge the fact that that any deficiency in their weather, attractions or digestible food is more than compensated for by the hospitality and warmth of the local population. Unfortunately Finland fails in this respect too. Finns (and it's hard to take a race seriously when they're named after part of a fish) have a reputation for being dour and solemn; guarded and serious. Spend an evening in a bar and you'll soon understand the irony of the local expression 'to be as talkative as a Finn'. Even trying to cause offence by calling them Scandinavian instead of Nordic on purpose will at best just provoke a raised eyebrow.

Interestingly, the Finnish language has no actual future tense; this is not surprising when you realise there's actually nothing to look forward to.

FIVE ABSOLUTELY TRUE FACTS ABOUT FINLAND
(NONE OF WHICH WILL INSPIRE YOU TO VISIT)

★ Finland is known officially as the Land of a Thousand Lakes (even though there are actually 187,000 of them).

★ It's been an independent nation for less than a hundred years. Some British supermarkets have been in existence longer.

★ There is no word for 'please' in the Finnish language.

★ The Finnish radio station Nuntii Latini broadcasts news in Latin.

★ There are annual wife-carrying and mosquito-swatting contests.

The sauna: enshrined in the Finnish identity (and everyone else's vocabulary)

The sauna is not just an integral part of Finnish society; the actual word is Finland's sole contribution to the global vocabulary. They have a saying: 'First you build a sauna then you build a house.' Good advice if you want to relax and refresh yourself; bad advice if you're homeless. Taking a sauna is as natural to Finns as breathing, although with sauna temperatures from 80°C to 100°C the breathing is usually very laboured. The Finns use saunas to relieve stress, burn calories and as a social ritual. It's difficult to know what causes newcomers more discomfort when they experience a sauna for the first time: meeting friends and neighbours while stark naked, or having them hit you with wet birch leaves.

HELSINKI

You know you're not off to a promising start when the best accolade bestowed on this city by guidebooks is that it's 'Europe's most walkable capital'. Helsinki is also described as 'the city where trends begin' although it's difficult to think of any … unless you consider the trend for 'not having much to see or do' in which case it justifies this sobriquet. Located on the southern coast, Helsinki is surrounded on three sides by water. Visitors who wish to save future generations from heartache and disappointment can only hope for a rapid increase in the rate of global warming so the capital can be surrounded on *all* sides by water and then hopefully sunk beneath the icy Baltic Sea.

DID YOU KNOW?

★ Donald Duck comics were once banned in Finland because he didn't wear trousers.

★ The Finns are the world's highest consumers of coffee. Visit this uninspiring country and you too will need that amount of chemical stimulation just to stay awake.

Attractions to avoid

★ **Rock Church (Temppeliaukio Kirkko)** It's a church that's been carved out of a rock – or rather it's just a large hole in the side of a rock that was roofed over, consecrated and then filled with tourists. Notable for unbelievably officious staff who treat it less as a place of religious significance and more as a place where they can shout and be rude to visitors.

★ **Yrjonkadun Swimming Hall** Not many swimming baths live up to their reputation as a major tourist attraction; this is one of them. Don't let the fact the venue is described as 'a cathedral of water sports' put you off visiting; you'll have many other reasons to avoid it instead. These include the nude single-sex swimming, cold water, no lane discipline and rude locals who treat all visitors as if they are verruca-ridden lepers.

★ **Finnish Parliament (Eduskuntatalo)** The seat of the Finnish government looks like it was designed by someone who wanted to see if he could combine the worst excess of Egyptian and Nazi-era style architecture. The authorities call this building 'imposing and solemn'. You'll call it 'pompous and hideous'.

★ **Seurasaari Open-Air Museum** On this island just outside the capital you can walk around cottages, farmsteads and manors from the past four centuries; at the time of writing there are eighty-seven separate buildings to explore. A must for those who want an insight into historic Finnish life or for whom life has lost all purpose.

MANY A TRUE WORD IS SPOKEN IN JEST

Q: How do you spot an extrovert Finn?
A: When talking to you, he stares at your feet instead of his own.

Other places to avoid

FINNISH LAPLAND

If you thought Finland was a wilderness then this most northerly region of Finland is a wasteland. Located almost entirely within the Arctic Circle it's home to the indigenous nomadic Sámi people. Guidebooks say that discovering their way of life can be as exciting and enriching as experiencing the Arctic north itself. It's not; there's only so much you can find interesting about reindeer herding.

Lapland is far better known as being the 'official home' of Santa Claus. Each winter the town of Rovaniemi is packed with shrieking middle class children from all across Europe who are visiting the Santa Claus Village. Gaudy, commercialised and tacky, this is basically an expensive shopping mall that just happens to have a Santa theme. In an effort to defend it against claims that this attraction is expensive, shameful and exploitative, the organisers say children will remember their experience here for the rest of their lives. The same could have been said about a Victorian workhouse.

Useful Finnish phrases

★ I'm sorry but I mistook your silence and reflection as a sign of rudeness and disrespect.
Olen pahoillani, mutta en luuli sinun hiljaisuus ja pohdintaa merkiksi röyhkeyden ja halveksuntaa.

★ Do you know any jokes at all that don't begin: 'There was this man from Sweden ...'?
Tiedättekö mitään vitsejä ollenkaan, jotka eivät ala: 'Oli tämä mies Ruotsista ...'?

★ When I asked for something refreshing I was thinking about a beer; I do not want you to take me swimming in a lake topped with a frozen crust of ice.
Kun kysyin jotain virkistävää Ajattelin olutta, en halua teitä ottamaan minut uida järven päällä jäädytetty kuori jäätä

Five reasons you know you're in Finland

❶ It's impossible to sit through a film or restaurant meal uninterrupted
Finland, home to Nokia, has one of the highest mobile phone penetration rates in Europe, with nearly 1.5 phones per head of the population. What's worse is that most of them have that bloody irritating Nokia ring tone.

❷ **Smiling is not common, nor is it encouraged** Smile at someone in the street and they'll automatically assume you are a) simple, b) drunk or c) a sexual predator.

❸ **You'll think you're in Stepford not Helsinki** There's a massive amount of conformity not just in how Finns think, but in the way they talk, dress, socialise and respect authority. Reckless lawbreaking usually involves someone crossing the road before the green man starts flashing.

❹ **The most popular confectionery tastes like stinging nettles** Salmiakki is an extremely salty liquorice that's a sal ammoniac. This is a substance that can be found as a white encrustation around volcanic fissures or dead batteries and is also used as a soldering flux. Salmiakki is described as an acquired taste; now you know why.

❺ **You'll be used to saying, 'No I don't want a second helping thank you.'** Sautéed reindeer, cow's head and hoof stew, and blood dumpling soup. The Finns have a very different understanding of the phrase 'simple and nourishing'.

FRANCE

The French are sawed-off sissies who eat snails and slugs and cheese that smells like people's feet. Utter cowards who force their own children to drink wine, they gibber like baboons even when you try to speak to them in their own wimpy language.

P. J. O'Rourke

IT'S SAID THAT the French aren't rude, they're busy.

That's a barefaced lie on two counts. Firstly a penchant for over-long lunch breaks, holidaying for the whole of August and going on strike at the drop of a chapeau means they're obviously not busy at all.

Secondly, French rudeness is there for all to see and hear in a variety of different ways. Take the Gallic shrug for example; a way of saying 'Up yours' without having to speak. Then there's the French custom of pretending not to understand English when they clearly do (often accompanied by the Gallic shrug).

However, the greatest example of French rudeness manifests itself in their sheer arrogance. With delusions of grandeur the French call their country La Grande Nation, chose the cock as their national emblem, and truly believe they invented not just the guillotine and the bidet but also food, wine, sex and fashion. They live on their past glories and hang on, limpet-like, to what remains of their far-flung colonies (just so they can use them for nuclear testing). And when it comes down to individuals, most French men think they're God's gift to women and most French women think they're God's gift to fashion designers. It's no surprise, then, to learn that Horace Walpole, the Fourth Earl of Orford, described the French as having 'insolent and unfounded airs of superiority'.

This conceit and feeling of self-importance is particularly rife in the service industry. Given that British visitors are generally resented and treated like *merde*, it's a wonder why anyone would ever want to visit in the first place.

As it's often said, the best thing between England and France is the sea.

Did you Know?

★ Not surprisingly, Mr Rude from the *Mr Men* TV series has a French accent.

★ Great Britain's overwhelming success in wars fought against France since 1066 (winning twenty-three, losing eleven) resulted in the French being nicknamed 'cheese eating surrender monkeys' and the saying 'Raise your right hand if you like the French ... Raise both hands if you are French.'

★ The French were the main supporters of the concept of European unity and the establishment of the EU.

★ France has the highest proportion of underweight women in Western Europe.

★ It's illegal to name a pig Napoleon in France.

PARIS

Everything unpleasant about France is accentuated in the capital. It's difficult to think of inhabitants of a city who are more snobbish or condescending. People also say that Parisians always seem to be in a rush; that's true ... well, apart from the waiters. A recent survey found that in London eateries it takes an average of 3.4 minutes to get a glass of water once a waiter has been alerted; in Paris it takes 17.9 minutes and when you complain they just shrug and say, 'C'est le vie . . .'. Apart from bad service there are several other reasons to avoid the French capital:

★ Paris is not the city of love, it's the city of dog poo (Parisians have difficulty understanding that there's a link between dog ownership and the concept of responsibility).

★ It makes London look positively cheap.

★ Statistically it rains more in Paris than in London.

★ The lighting on the Paris Metro makes everyone look like an extra in *Dawn of the Dead*.

★ If you ask a sales assistant in department store for help they'll automatically refer you to another floor … just to get rid of you.

★ One third of Parisians smoke.

★ Parisians go the longest time without baths or showers, and have one of the lowest levels of soap consumption per capita.

★ Paris is so unpleasant that it's given its name to an actual psychological disorder: Paris Syndrome. This affects people visiting Paris and is characterised by a number of psychiatric symptoms including perceptions of being a victim of prejudice, aggression or hostility.

★ Jean-Paul Sartre said, 'Hell is other people.' He was wrong. Hell is Parisians.

THE FRENCH: LIVING IN THE PAST

Proof of France's obsession with past glories is the fact that the French language has seven different past tenses including the pluperfect of the indicative, the past anterior and the past subjunctive. How many ways do you need to refer to something that's already happened?

Attractions to avoid

★ **Musée du Louvre** Everyone knows the Louvre, one of the world's largest museums that's housed in an old Parisian palace dating back to the twelfth-century. Recognised the world over for the large glass pyramid that stands in its main courtyard and its abysmally sluggish ticket office, the Louvre displays 35,000 works of art. However 78% of visitors just go to see one: the 'Mona Lisa'. If you follow in their footsteps, prepare to be disappointed. The portrait is tiny; not just because it's far smaller than you think but because there's always a ten-deep crowd in front of you preventing you getting close. Mona Lisa's smile was enigmatic. Your crestfallen expression will be very obvious.

★ **River Seine** An evening stroll along the banks of the Seine sounds enchanting. The reality is that you'll be pestered by intimidating beggars and shouted at by drunken vagrants; neither of these experiences could in any way be described as captivating or romantic. The river itself is brown and dirty and, apart from the Eiffel Tower, none of the monuments or historic buildings that line the Seine are illuminated. Take an evening riverboat cruise and you might as well be anywhere (except the staff on the boat will be rude and unhelpful, so you'll know you're still in Paris.)

★ **Notre Dame Cathedral** Described as a masterpiece of twelfth-century Gothic architecture this cathedral is less about spirituality and more about souvenir stands, gift shops, vending machines and what appears to be a small flea market selling religious items. The shuffling tsunami of tourists trying to get in and out has turned this into an experience similar to waiting in line to pay at the supermarket, albeit slightly less fun.

★ **Eiffel Tower** Only worth seeing from a distance. If you decide to travel up the Eiffel Tower be prepared for security that's slow and disorganised, lifts that travel (appropriately enough) at a snail's pace and an observation deck that's dirty and cramped. When you do reach the top the view is disappointing. Paris is sprawling and grey and the novelty of the panorama will start to decay almost immediately. The French idea of irony is evident here; an abundance of signs that warn against pickpockets but acute overcrowding that makes their job simple.

★ **Sacre-Coeur (Sacred Heart Basilica of Montmartre)** This sits at the highest point in Paris on the hill of Montmartre. After looking around the church and looking out over an uninspiring view of Paris that consists mainly of roof tops, you'll still have time to be pestered by North African vendors selling gold-looking bracelets, wind-up flying birds, badly carved wooden camels and assorted other *merde*.

Montmartre is the artistic quarter where you can watch failed artists at work producing production-line quality paintings. Alternatively, you can stop in one of the cafés that line the main square behind the Sacre-Coeur and assist the French economy by paying £5 for a glass of Coke.

★ **Centre Pompidou** This performance and exhibition space divides opinion. There are those who think it's an architectural masterpiece. There are those who think it's an architectural monstrosity. And there are those who think it's a soulless, unwelcoming attraction that perpetually sells more tickets than its capacity allows without any regard to queue lengths, making it one of the best examples of Parisian greed and disorganisation. Not so much Pompidou as Pompidon't.

★ **Arc de Triomphe** It's just an archway. Get over it.

★ **Pigalle** A typical evening in the Pigalle involves being enticed into one of the seedy strip clubs by a €10 admission fee that promises a free drink. Next thing you know, a skinny topless girl wearing tatty knickers brings you two opened bottles of cheap champagne and you're presented with a bill for €400. The rest of the night involves a stand-off with a hulking Moroccan holding a baseball bat followed by being roughed up by two bouncers until you 'negotiate' an appropriate exit fee.

FIVE ABSOLUTELY TRUE FACTS ABOUT FRANCE
(NONE OF WHICH WILL INSPIRE YOU TO VISIT)

★ According to a recent survey, only 47% of French people take a daily bath or shower (compared to 70% of the British).
★ They do however take more suppositories than the whole of Europe combined.
★ That Jerry Lewis was awarded the Légion d'Honneur confirms that the French have no sense of humour; in fact, the word 'humour' did not officially enter the French language until 1932.
★ With approximately 25% people working for local or central government, France is the most bureaucratic country in the world, with almost twice as many civil servants as Germany.
★ The croissant was invented in Austria, French fries originated in Belgium while French toast owes its origins to a recipe from fourth-century Rome.

Other places in France to avoid

★ **Provence** Forests, vineyards, olive groves, medieval hilltop villages, smelly food markets, thermal baths and artistic glassware ... You'll be bored to tears after a few hours, let alone a whole year.
★ **Lourdes** The miracle of Lourdes is not so much that Bernadette Soubirous saw a vision of the Virgin Mary here in 1858, but how the town has managed to con so many people into visiting it since then. Don't come here if you want a cure for cancer. Do come here if you want to buy a plastic Madonna.
★ **Marseilles** Located on the southeast coast, Marseilles is the second largest city in France and offers visitors everything they'd associate with a bustling cosmopolitan port: racial tension, street crime, low level drug dealers, rife alcoholism, cheap prostitutes, gang fights and police on the take.

★ **The French Riviera (Nice, Monaco, Cannes, St Tropez)** This area is known as the Theatre of Life … the problem is that you'll only be able to afford a seat at the back with an obstructed view.

USEFUL PHRASES TO USE IN FRANCE

★ How many different types of cheese do you actually need?
De combien de types de fromage avez-vous réellement besoin?

★ I am aware that Albert Camus said, 'I know of only one duty, and that is to love' but that does not give you the automatic right to put your hand on my wife's bottom.
Je suis conscient qu'Albert Camus disait: «Je ne connais qu'un seul devoir, et c'est à l'amour», mais cela ne vous donne pas automatiquement le droit de mettre la main sur les fesses de ma femme.

★ Thank you but I do not want to purchase a beret. Why would I want any headwear that was modelled on a cowpat?
Merci, mais je ne veux pas acheter un béret. Pourquoi voudrais-je un couvre-chef qui a été calqué sur une bouse de vache?

Five reasons you know you're in France

❶ **Lunch isn't just a meal, it's a period of time** It's no wonder that nothing gets done in France. Lunch breaks on workdays tend to last three hours and are always fuelled by a couple of bottles of cheap Merlot. In an effort to defend this practice the French claim they use the time to talk about work; technically this is true however the topics usually involve blockading ports or taking industrial action.

❷ **Napoleon is omnipresent** Over 200 French streets, institutions and monuments celebrate this French dictator and megalomaniac, a man whose greatest legacy was lending his name to a psychological phenomenon involving aggressive behaviour in short men.

❸ **Music that's as derivative as it is horrendous** In France music hasn't just stood still, it's actually moved backwards. Think of what was popular a decade ago and you'll hear a pale imitation of it nowadays on French radio and TV. Two of France's best known music stars are Johnny Hallyday, a man perhaps better known for plastic surgery than musical talent, and Yannick Noah, the ex-Tennis player better at holding a racquet than a tune.

❹ **Everyone moans (and not in a sexy Jane Birkin way)** French people are never happier than when they're complaining about something. From 1789 onwards, protests, demonstrations and other acts of civil disobedience have been as natural to the French as their cavalier attitude towards personal hygiene. Even Napoleon said, 'The French complain of everything, and always.'

❺ **No one likes you** Don't take it personally. The French are very insular (even worse than the Japanese) and dislike and distrust most foreigners … but especially the British, Americans and Belgians. Parisians, however, take narrow-mindedness to the extreme. Not only do they look down on anyone who doesn't live in the capital, they also have utter contempt for other Parisians.

FRENCH CUISINE: ANYTHING GOES

The French like to think that their cuisine is refined and superior and that they're discerning when it comes to what they eat. The reality is that they are actually the least fussy nation on the planet. The French will eat anything that crawls, hops, walks, runs, gallops, swims, flies or leaves a slimy trail behind it. They're also fond of eating animal parts that most other nations turn their noses up at – and this includes noses (well, snouts anyway), ears, tails, hoofs, brains, entrails and reproductive organs.

PEOPLE SAY THE NICEST THINGS ABOUT FRANCE . . .

France has neither winter, summer, nor morals – apart from these drawbacks, it is a fine country.
Mark Twain

How can one conceive of a one party system in a country that has over 200 varieties of cheese?
Charles de Gaulle

Basically the French are all peasants.
Pablo Picasso

The French are a logical people, which is one reason the English dislike them so intensely. The other is that they own France, a country which we have always judged to be much too good for them.
Robert Morley

France is a country where the money falls apart but you can't tear the toilet paper.
Billy Wilder

I would rather have a German division in front of me than a French one behind me.
General George S. Patton

Going to war without France is like going deer hunting without your accordion.
Norman Schwartzkopf

You know, the French remind me a little bit of an aging actress of the 1940s who is still trying to dine out on her looks but doesn't have the face for it.
Senator John McCain

They've taken their own precautions against Al Qaeda. To prepare for an attack, each Frenchman is urged to keep duct tape, a white flag and a three-day supply of mistresses in the house.
Argus Hamilton

I would call the French scumbags, but that, of course, would be a disservice to bags filled with scum.

Dennis Miller

You know why the French don't want to bomb Saddam Hussein? Because he hates America, he loves mistresses and wears a beret. He IS French, people.

Conan O'Brien

If the French were really intelligent, they'd speak English.

Wilfrid Sheed

The French: Germans with good food.

Fran Lebowitz

France: ever wanted to slap an entire country?

Steve Landesburg

They are a short, blue-vested people who carry their own onions when cycling abroad, and have a yard which is 3.37 inches longer than other people's.

Alan Coren

Attila, the scourge of God; the French, his brothers.

Italian saying

The friendship of the French is like their wine: exquisite, but of short duration.

German saying

Paris is like a whore: from a distance she seems ravishing, you can't wait until you have her in your arms. Five minutes later you feel empty, disgusted with yourself. You feel tricked.

Henry Miller

When the Frenchman sleeps, the devil rocks him.

French saying

A fighting Frenchman runs away from even a she-goat.

Russian saying

GARLIC: NATURE'S ABOMINATION

> Do not eat garlic or onions; for their smell
> will reveal that you are a peasant.
> *Cervantes, Don Quixote*

VISIT ANY SOUTHERN European country and you'll discover that the only animal-based food without garlic in it is an egg with its shell intact (although it's believed EU scientists are working on this oversight).

Garlic, or to give it its Latin name *allium sativum* (literally, 'vile aftertaste'), has a long history in European cuisine after chefs in France, Spain, Portugal and Italy first discovered its most valuable property: its ability to disguise the taste of nauseating Mediterranean dishes.

In addition to this essential role in European cuisine, garlic lovers maintain that the vegetable has considerable health benefits, calling it 'nature's pharmacy', and claiming it lowers blood pressure and cholesterol. Then again, garlic is meant to ward off vampires so it's probably best to ignore any supposed health benefits as mythological mumbo-jumbo.

Garlic lovers acknowledge that the vegetable does have its critics and compare it to Marmite. This paints an inaccurate view about garlic; it's actually more like raw liver. Everyone hates it.

Garlic FAQs

★ *What are the main properties of garlic?*
Its role in birth control.

★ *What does eating raw garlic taste like?*
Licking a live battery.

★ *Does garlic have a place in the kitchen?*
Yes. Under or behind somewhere heavy and inaccessible like the fridge or the saucepan cabinet.

★ *What's worse than the smell of garlic?*
Its taste.

★ *I heard that the slaves who built the pyramids in Ancient Egypt chewed on garlic to give them energy.*
You're an idiot.

GERMANY

The best thing you can say about Germany is that
since 1990 there's only been one of them.

Anonymous

HUN, FRITZ, JERRY, Kraut, Boche, Squarehead, Herman, Sausage
Eater, Rhine Monkey … The Germans have one of the highest
numbers of derogatory nicknames in the world – even beating
the French (and that's quite an achievement).

Why then is there so much hostility towards the country? Numerous
social studies have attempted to pinpoint the underlying reasons and their
conclusions are surprising. It must be said that in the last hundred years
the Germans have not been particularly popular in Europe (or throughout
the world for that matter), mainly for starting two world wars. Then there's
Germany's spectacular phoenix-like rise from the ashes of bombed cities
into a nation that's become the economic powerhouse of Europe – and
the strongest advocate of the EU ideal. Don't forget, too, Germany's
reputation for designing and manufacturing some of the best cars in the
world, their illustrious achievements in the arts, literature and science and
the persistent success in Europe of their football clubs.

While all these are valid, the main reasons Germany is disliked so
much nowadays comes down to two factors that directly affect visitors.

The first is the food. It's truly so bad that even Hitler was a
vegetarian. Go into a restaurant and the waiter will say something like,

'Would you like some schupfnudeln with your sauerbraten?' How appetising is that?

The second reason is the language, which has been described as being extravagantly ugly; even a simple sentence sounds like someone using an in-flight sick bag. German is not a language that's comfortable expressing affection or being funny; instead it's particularly well suited to shouting orders.

And on the subject of language, only the Germans could have invented the concept of *schadenfreude,* the pleasure derived from the misfortunes of others.

And by 'others', they mean anyone visiting Germany.

DID YOU KNOW?

★ The Germans' reputation for efficiency is a result of an indoctrination that begins at a very early age. One of the songs taught to young children is: 'Morgen morgen nur nicht heute sagen alle faule leute,' meaning, 'Tomorrow, tomorrow, not today is what all the lazy people say.'

★ Munich's huge annual beer festival is Oktoberfest but it starts in September. So much for German efficiency ... or calendars.

BERLIN

Germany is full of regulations but one of the most rigorously enforced is the unwritten rule that says you have to love Berlin, a capital that presents itself as the coolest, buzziest city in Europe. Berliners say, 'What's not to like?' Everyone else says, 'Where do I start?' To be fair, Berlin does have a certain appeal – but that appeal is limited to those who like discourteous locals, ugly graffiti, abandoned buildings, heroin addicts, mind-numbing electronic music, pseudo-intellectual hipsters, racial tension and streets filled with the detritus of clubbers.

Attractions to avoid

★ **Memorial of the Berlin Wall** At 96 miles long and 12 feet high the original Berlin Wall was big; now it's just a big disappointment. There's hardly any of the original wall left and what remains is less of a memorial to the dark history of this divided city and more of a chewing gum depository. To truly experience and understand the brutality of the Cold War era visit the Information Centre, where all the staff seem to be ex-border guards.

★ **Berlin Wall Museum (Museum Haus am Checkpoint Charlie)** Those coming here to learn more about the history of the Berlin Wall will be frustrated and/or confused. Many displays are out of date, yellowing and incomprehensible, seemingly translated by someone for whom English was not their first language ... and neither was German. Add to this an extortionate entrance fee and a series of small, hot, overcrowded museum rooms and you'll find yourself drawing on the improvisational skills and courage of the successful escapees.

★ **Brandenburg Gate** This former eighteenth-century City Gate commissioned by King Frederick William II of Prussia is now considered by many to be the primary symbol of Berlin's rich and turbulent history. They are wrong. It's more of a primary symbol of Berlin's ability to over-restore one of its historic attractions so that it looks like it was built two years ago. Come here only if you want to have your photo taken with out-of-work actors posing as Russian soldiers or to buy smelly currywurst sausages from unhygienic-looking food carts.

★ **Alexanderplatz** In the 1970s this area of East Berlin became an experiment in socialist urban aesthetics. A more accurate description is 'Commie concrete jungle'. A sterile, dismal, cold, depressing hell-hole ... it's difficult to think of a more perfect place to commit suicide.

★ **Reichstag** Opened in 1894 this is the home of the German Parliament and is best known for the incredibly torturous and inefficient way that you have to buy tickets online three days in advance, a security screening system that treats each visitor as if they are a blood relative of Ulrike Meinhoff and some of the most unknowledgeable staff to ever work in a tourist attraction. In June 1995 environmental artist Christo wrapped the Reichstag completely in fabric. The tragedy is that a month later he unwrapped it.

MUNICH

A rich heritage of extremist politics, Hitler's failed coup and the subsequent epicentre of the Nazi movement … Munich has forgotten many things in its long, sordid past. However visitors today will discover the city's collective amnesia also extends to how to provide value for money and anything of real interest. So-called attractions include:

★ **The BMW Museum:** a haven for those interested in bad caféteria food and staff as discourteous as most BMW drivers.

★ **Olympiapark:** the only reason to go here would have been in 1972 when it was home to the Olympics. Forty years later you'll experience a desolate venue with a crumbling infrastructure and general air of neglect.

★ **Oktoberfest:** Munich's version of the Mardi Gras but with less parades, floats and jazz and more overcrowding, aggressive behaviour, obesity, drunkenness, insincere camaraderie, forced jollity and an all-pervasive back-alley stench of stale alcohol.

FRANKFURT

Visitors to Germany will be surprised to learn there are, in fact, two Frankfurts – probably a ruse to confuse Allied bombers in the Second World War. One is boringly provincial and is called Frankfurt an der Oder. The other is Frankfurt-am-Main and is slightly less boring. As the country's financial centre, it gained the nickname 'Bankfurt' in a stunning demonstration of astute German wit. What isn't amusing however is how disappointed you'll be walking around attractions that include:

★ **Frankfurter Roemer:** the site of Frankfurt's city hall since 1405, most of the square was destroyed in the war but rather than improve the city, the old houses were rebuilt to form a phoney tourist backdrop. More of a film set than a historic square.

★ **Berger Strasse:** the longest shopping street in Frankfurt conjures up images of select boutiques along its almost two-mile length. In reality it's full of mediocre shops including a large Woolworths. Berger Strasse dates back to the middle ages; so does the retail experience.

★ **Dialog Museum:** small groups are led through various rooms in pitch darkness by a blind guide, having to rely on their senses to explore various exhibits. While the idea of being able to understand the world of the blind is commendable, visitors should be prepared to be felt up on the way round or short-changed in the café.

FIVE ABSOLUTELY TRUE FACTS ABOUT GERMANY
(NONE OF WHICH WILL INSPIRE YOU TO VISIT)

★ Most German food is expensive or makes you fat. Or both.
★ The döner kebab was invented in West Berlin in 1971
★ David Hasselhoff is still big in Germany and has had two number one records.
★ Known as Hitler's tailor, Hugo Boss designed the official uniforms for the Nazi Party and the Hitler Youth.
★ Munich's motto is 'München mag dich', which means 'Munich likes you'. It doesn't. It likes your money.

HAMBURG

There's a saying in Hamburg, 'die Wolken sind Hamburger Sonne', which means 'the clouds are Hamburg's sun'. But not only is the weather dull, so is Hamburg itself. You'd assume that a sprawling German city that's home to one of the biggest harbours in Europe would be lively but

Hamburg defies expectations. The metro and restaurants close earlier than in most northern European cities and apart from the red-light district where it's still possible to get stabbed at 3 a.m., the nightlife is also disappointing. It's no surprise then that Hamburg is known as 'The city that always sleeps'. See if you can stay awake when you visit these so-called attractions:

★ **Rathaus:** Not literally a house of rats but the nineteenth-century city hall – although a house full of rats would be far more appealing. You can take a forty-minute guided tour, learning about Hamburg's political history, although this is not suitable for those who have trouble with stairs or staying awake.

★ **Alter Elbtunnel:** This 1,400-foot-long tunnel beneath the River Elbe should be treated not as a tourist attraction but simply as a way to reach the other side, if you really want to.

★ **Reeperbahn:** If you disapprove of red-light districts you'll be vindicated. If you approve of red-light districts you'll be disappointed. If you like seeing ugly hookers, aggressive pimps, seedy sex shops, cheap peep shows, hostile drug addicts, salmonella-ridden fast food restaurants, squalid strip clubs, vomit-encrusted pavements, discarded syringes, and legions of pickpockets and beggars, the Reeperbahn is the ideal place for you.

Other places to avoid

BAVARIA

Oompah bands, beer halls, lederhosen, sausages and right-wing leanings masquerading as a traditional way of life … you'll find all of the German stereotypes in Bavaria. If you only have time to visit one place in Germany during your stay, make sure it's not here.

USEFUL PHRASES TO USE IN GERMANY

★ I didn't realise that you found punctuality such a turn-on.
Mir war nicht bewusst, dass Sie gefunden Pünktlichkeit wie ein Turn-on.

★ Please stop the yodelling and slapping dances. I have a severe headache.
Bitte beenden Sie die Jodler und slapping Tänze. Ich habe eine starke Kopfschmerzen.

★ I find it difficult to understand how a nation that gave the word Nietzsche, Goethe and Kant now holds David Hasselhoff in such high esteem.
Ich finde es schwierig zu verstehen, wie eine Nation, die das Wort Nietzsche, Goethe und Kant gab jetzt hält David Hasselhoff in so hoher Wertschätzung.

Five reasons you know you're in Germany

❶ **An anally retentive approach to punctuality** Saying 'I'll be back about four' is as alien to most Germans as saying 'Tell me a joke'. A careful analysis of travel times enables Germans to pinpoint arrangements to precise times like 10.27 or 17.53. And when they say 17.53 they get very disappointed if you arrive at 17.54.

❷ **Beer is not so much a drink as a way of life** Germany is the largest consumer of beer in Europe, with over 5,000 brands to choose from. In Bavaria a beer glass holds two pints and they take the concept of a liquid lunch quite literally since beer there is officially classed as a food.

❸ **Getting served in a bakery can take hours** There are about 300 varieties of bread in Germany. Not good news if you have an indecisive customer ahead of you in the queue, or if you are gluten intolerant.

❹ **You'll hear some of the most annoying music in the world** There's no point in changing radio stations when a techno record comes on since the next five German stations you tune in to will also be playing techno. Many people confuse techno with the genres 'synth-pop' or 'trance'. Many more confuse it with the genre 'music'.

⑤ **You'll find pornography on sale next to children's magazines** Germans have a very liberal attitude not only towards the content of pornographic magazines but also towards where the magazines are displayed. Go into supermarkets or petrol stations and expect to find a copy of *Übergrossen Busen* rubbing shoulders (and other parts) with *Micky Maus*.

PEOPLE SAY THE NICEST THINGS ABOUT GERMANY . . .

One German, a beer; two Germans, an organization;
three Germans, a war.
Polish saying

The German may be a good fellow, but it is best to hang
him just the same.
Russian saying

One thing I will say about the Germans; they are always perfectly
willing to give somebody's land to somebody else.
Will Rogers

God invented man, the devil invented the German.
Polish saying

Life is too short to learn German.
Richard Porson

The German mind has a talent for making no mistakes but the very
greatest.
Clifton Fadiman

German is a language which was developed solely to afford the speaker
the opportunity to spit at strangers under the guise of polite
conversation.
National Lampoon

I speak Spanish to God, Italian to women, French to men and
German to my horse.
Emperor Charles V

Three things are in trouble: birds in the hands of children, young girls
in the hands of old men and wine in the hands of Germans.
Italian saying

A dead German, a dead dog; the difference is but slight.
Polish saying

Rather Turkish hatred than German love.

Croatian saying

You will sooner catch a ray of the sun than reach an agreement with a German.

Polish saying

GREECE

After shaking hands with a Greek, count your fingers.
Albanian saying

IF GREECE EVER wrote its autobiography it would be called 'How The Mighty Have Fallen' or 'That Was Then, This is Now'. Of course, Greece would never write its own autobiography. Not because the concept of an entire sovereign state writing something down is an unfeasible, abstract concept, but because nowadays it can't afford any pens or notepads.

It's ironic that a country that is considered to be the birthplace of Western civilisation, creating fundamental new ideas in education, government, science, art, architecture and philosophy, has now almost been reduced to the status of 'developing nation'. Like its pitiful Mediterranean neighbour Cyprus, this is a country teetering on the brink of total financial collapse, with a public debt binge that's been spiralling out of control since 2007 and which, at the time of writing, was approximately €300 billion.

Taking enough factor-20 suncream and a substantial supply of Imodium is no longer the biggest concern of holidaymakers. Ruthless austerity measures, depression-levels of recession, the possible introduction of an 'emergency drachma' worth only about 10% of the euro, airlines or hotels that might cease trading overnight and a general fear of strikes and political unrest have meant that Greece is no longer such an attractive proposition for visitors (nor, it must be said, its inhabitants).

The first Greek tragedy was performed in 534 BC. It's a performance that still plays out today.

Greece's Olympic legacy

If you want to visit any of the impressive stadiums and sporting venues developed for the 2004 Athens Games you'll be in for an Olympic-sized disappointment. The legacy of the €9 billion spent on the games is that many of the thirty-six venues upgraded or built from scratch lie dilapidated. Some have become gypsy squatter camps or dumping grounds for waste, while most just lie derelict. If the shameful abuse of public money was an Olympic sport, the Greeks would be gold medal holders.

ATHENS

The Greek tourist authority claims that the capital Athens is 'undergoing a difficult period of urban renewal'. However, visitors should be aware this phrase is in fact a euphemism for 'we've run out of money to repair the roads, maintain public transport or municipal buildings'.

It also promotes the fact that there are no cars in Athens' historic centre although this should not be seen as a progressive environmental measure but rather just the consequence that locals can no longer afford to run cars (many experience extreme financial hardship just filling up the windscreen washer bottle).

Athens has always been promoted as a more sophisticated, conspicuously wealthier city. These days, though, conspicuous wealth is anyone flaunting a takeaway latte or possessing matching shoes.

* The Greek wine *retsina* has a taste that can only be compared to pine scented Toilet Duck.
* The economy means that restaurants rarely let customers smash plates nowadays. Or if they do, they ensure they have an ample supply of superglue.
* Around 500 BC Greece introduced what has become recognised as the Western world's first municipal dump. This has since expanded to become the whole country.

Attractions to avoid

★ **The Acropolis** The word 'ruins' or indeed 'sacred rock' have never been the biggest tourist 'come-ons' and such it is with the Acropolis. Rising above the city, it contains the remains of several ancient temples, the most famous being the Parthenon. The Greeks have the same concept of ticketing and organisation as they do of responsible government expenditure or paying taxes, so to get to the top you need to survive a ill-tempered queue with no shade, an hour's wait for tickets and at least a thirty-minute dangerously overcrowded trek. If you do make it to the top without suffering heatstroke or a fist fight with Turkish tourists cutting in line, walking around will give you more of an appreciation of modern scaffolding than ancient structures.

★ **Temple of Athena Nike** An attempt by the Greek tourist authority to mislead visitors into thinking this is some sort of outlet mall. It isn't and there's no shop selling postcards, let alone Air Jordans.

★ **Temple of Hephaestus** Slightly more underwhelming than the Panthenon.

★ **Erechtheion** Another old temple.

★ **Temple of Olympian Zeus** Yawn.

★ **Odeum of Herodes Atticus** Kill me now.

★ **Hadrian's Arch** It's just a stone arch. The lower half is Roman and the top is Greek. Whoopie-Doo.

THE GREEK ISLANDS

Corfu, Crete, Santorini, Skiathos, Mykonos, Rhodes, Patmos, Hydra, Lemnos, Samos, Naxos, Thassos, Icaria, Paros, Pistros, Lesbos, Kastos, Pontikos, Andros … the list goes on and on and on. And on. Even the Greeks themselves can't be bothered to find how many inhabited islands there are, with estimates ranging from 166 to 227. To be honest it's not worth the time or effort in differentiating between them as they all promise visitors the exact same things:

★ **sandy beaches**
★ **rustic tavernas**
★ **unspoilt surroundings**
★ **picturesque countryside**
★ **lesbians***

*Okay, only Lesbos promises this but it's nice to fantasise.

MALIA, CRETE: PARTY CENTRAL

The promise sounds good: *the* destination for sunshine, binge drinking and casual sex. However, the reality tends to be rather different. Most visitors to Malia will wake up not in the bed of a complete stranger but in the local A&E after falling off a quad bike or from an eighth floor balcony, or in Heraklion Central Court charged with fighting the locals or mooning at the police.

Crete was once known as the place where seven virgins were sacrificed to the minotaur; but that was back when virgins were plentiful.

FIVE ABSOLUTELY TRUE FACTS ABOUT GREECE
(NONE OF WHICH WILL INSPIRE YOU TO VISIT)

* The words 'economic' and 'chaos' both derive from the Greek ('okionomia' and 'khaos'). No surprises there.
* Greece is the leading producer of sea sponges and the fifth largest exporter of asparagus.
* In Ancient Greece the three biggest influences were Socrates, Plato and Aristotle; nowadays, it's the European Commission, the European Central Bank and the International Monetary Fund.
* 80% of the country is mountainous.
* Anything happening within an hour of the intended time is considered punctual.

Five reasons you know you're in Greece

❶ **The locals look reflective and studious** Nowadays though they're not getting to grips with trigonometry and algebra; they're calculating how they're going to survive on a 30% pay cut and no pension.

❷ **... and like their illustrious ancestors, they're very philosophical** These days though it's less about Plato's belief in the immortality of the soul and more about wondering how they're going to get through the rest of the week.

❸ **You'll probably get spat at** Not because the locals are rude, but just because spitting is part of their culture. When a Greek compliments someone on their good looks it's customary to spit on them three times to ward off the evil eye. At Greek Orthodox baptisms people spit three times to keep the devil away. And seeing shoes with the soles facing you is considered bad luck ... and is also warded off by guess what? That's right: spitting.

❹ It's easy to get a restaurant table reservation Brutal austerity measures mean that the locals can't afford to go out to eat (or indeed, to eat).

❺ The country might be called something different by the time you leave Some economists and political commentators have predicted that Greece will soon cease to exist as a sovereign state. Its debts will be bought by a major corporation and the country will be completely rebranded.

USEFUL PHRASES TO USE IN GREECE

★ Why do you blame everyone in the world for your financial woes except yourselves?
Γιατί φταίει ο καθένας στη λέξη, εκτός από τον εαυτό σας για τις οικονομικές θλίψεις σας;

★ Is that a two thousand year old historic monument or just a modern building that's been badly damaged by Molotov cocktails during anti-austerity riots?
Είναι ότι δύο χιλιάδες χρόνια παλιό ιστορικό μνημείο ή απλά ένα σύγχρονο κτίριο που είναι ήδη σοβαρές ζημιές από βόμβες μολότοφ κατά τη διάρκεια της αντι-λιτότητας εξεγέρσεις;

★ Your illustrious ancestors have given you an inflated sense of self-esteem and a completely unearned sense of superiority.
Επιφανείς πρόγονοί σας έχουν δώσει μια διογκωμένη αίσθηση της αυτοεκτίμησης και ένα εντελώς μη δεδουλευμένα αίσθηση της ανωτερότητας.

HUNGARY

Sins are born in Hungary.
Czech saying

A **TOURISM CAMPAIGN ONCE** used the theme 'Fungary' in a naïve attempt to promote the country as a cool 'happening' place to visit. Needless to say this was a dismal failure and proof once again that it's impossible to polish a turd (although many tourist boards have found it *is* possible to roll it around in glitter).

However hard the Hungarian authorities tried to repackage their country and promote all its natural and man-made attractions they found it difficult to shake off the country's reputation as a land of goulash, castle ruins, post-Communist architecture and a refusal among its locals to acknowledge the word 'hospitality'. The same campaign tried to give Hungary a more sophisticated air, positioning it in central rather than eastern Europe. The fact that it has a vibrant black market, gypsy violinists pestering you in restaurants, horse and carts and a national dress that resembles an explosion in an embroidery factory proves this geographic relocation lacked credibility.

So ... what is the main reason most visitors go Hungary today? The answer is dental work; Hungary is responsible for about 40% of the world's dental tourism. Forget 2,000 years of colourful history, the Carpathian mountains, a capital known as the Pearl of the Danube and the largest freshwater lake in Europe; today's visitors are more likely to visit Hungary for low-cost dental implants, zirconium crowns or ceramic veneers.

And when the prime reason to visit your country involves a degree of pain, numbness and general anaesthetic then the tourist office really does need to try a lot harder.

DID YOU KNOW?

★ Szépasszony Völgy, near the baroque city of Eger in northeastern Hungary, is famous for its wide range of regional wines. The area's name means 'The valley of the beautiful women'. You'll find this is only true after two or three bottles.

★ The Rubik's Cube was invented by Hungarian Ernő Rubik. There are 43,252,003,274,489,856,000 (forty-three quintillion) permutations … about the same number of reasons not to visit Hungary.

BUDAPEST

Hungary's capital is known as the Pearl of the Danube. However it's very unlikely that you'd find an oyster in the Danube since no living thing except virulent bacteria could survive in this toxic sludge hole. Nonetheless, the description is used to highlight Budapest's reputation as a sophisticated and cultural gem, offering a wide selection of baroque, neoclassical and art nouveau buildings in addition to a wealth of galleries, parks, spas and museums. However there's more to Budapest than architecture, the arts and history. Visitors will discover the city also has much to offer by way of graffiti, pollution, prostitution and organised crime.

Attractions to avoid

★ **The Danube** Johann Strauss II was a hopeless romantic (and chronically colour blind) when he composed his most famous waltz in 1866. The Danube cannot be described as 'blue' in any sense of the word. Even calling it dirty grey or brown is flattering. This river, which runs north–south and almost divides Hungary in two, has a history of contamination by fertilisers, pesticides, phosphates, nitrates and heavy metals and is therefore of more interest to scientists and ecological clean-up groups than swimmers.

As far as sightseeing goes, the Danube might be one of the most famous rivers in Europe but it's also the most inaccessible. There are no walkways or embankments by the river, just car parks and dual carriageways, so the only way to experience the river is by one of the many boat tours. If you're looking forward to ninety minutes of piped gypsy music, an incomprehensible commentary over the sound of loud engines and the all-pervasive smell of diesel fumes then you won't be disappointed.

★ **Margaret Island (Margitsziget)** The word 'attraction' is a hubristic claim for this recreational spot located in the Danube. Walking over an unremarkable bridge will probably be the most interesting part of your visit. Other features include a large park with neglected flowerbeds, bird excrement-encrusted monuments and an 'enchanting Japanese garden' that's anything but. Visitors can also experience an assortment of catering establishments of questionable hygiene.

★ **Buda Castle** Budapest has an extensive history but this thirteenth-century palace is not really part of it. The castle was destroyed and rebuilt so many times in its existence that no one can recognise any of the original walls or structures or knows what particular period it's actually been restored as. For 'historic charm' read 'complete lack of authenticity'.

★ **Heroes' Square** This was probably quite grand in 1896 when it was constructed to celebrate the 1,000th anniversary of the Magyar Conquest of Hungary. Nowadays it's more of a place to 'people watch', as long as the people you want to watch are gypsies begging, bored Hungarian youths skateboarding and menacing old men.

FIVE ABSOLUTELY TRUE FACTS ABOUT HUNGARY
(NONE OF WHICH WILL INSPIRE YOU TO VISIT)

★ Without paprika the country's cuisine would fail to exist.
★ The age of consent is fourteen.
★ It's traditional for Santa Claus (Mikulás) to be joined by one or two evil, threatening companions (Krampusz).
★ Not only is Hungarian one of the hardest languages to learn, the alphabet contains forty letters including fourteen vowels.
★ Many people tip doctors and petrol pump attendants.

Other places to avoid

★ **Lake Balaton** Located in the west of the country this 230 square mile freshwater lake is affectionately called 'The Hungarian Sea'. It is also less affectionately called 'a bit of a disappointment'.

★ **Thermal Lake of Hévíz** Situated at the western edge of Lake Balaton this facility features a spa house full of jostling, rude, fat tourists and a series of restaurants on a par with those you'd find in the food court of a motorway service station. When it comes to bad overpriced food and being leered at by sweaty sixty-year-old men while you wear a skimpy towel, this destination is hard to beat.

Five reasons you know you're in Hungary

① **You'll think that all the locals have acute gastroenteritis** Not only is Hungarian recognised as one of the most difficult languages in the world to master but also anyone speaking it sounds as though they are about to have an alien erupt from their belly.

❷ **The TV is confusing** The Hungarian state TV station is called MTV (Magyar Televízió) and broadcasts a staple diet of poor game shows and low budget soaps. This is probably not the MTV you're looking for.

❸ **Drinking bull's blood is preferable to drinking Bull's Blood** The country's famous red wine Bull's Blood (Bikavér) was popularised in the mid-eighteenth century as a medicine. One sip and you'll know why.

❹ **Fashion sensibilities that would cause even Lady Gaga to roll her eyes** Polyester animal print leggings, viscose crop tops, acrylic two-tone cardigans, nylon collarless shirts – all worn with flip-flops. Hungarian dress sense embodies a complete lack of understanding of the word style (or natural fibres).

❺ **You'll perpetually be saying, 'How much?!'** Hungary has the highest rate of VAT in Europe; a whacking great 27%. This makes prices in the UK look reasonable.

USEFUL HUNGARIAN PHRASES

★ It's not often that I meet staff who exude a combination of surliness with thinly veiled hostility.
Ez nem túl gyakran találkozom személyzet, hogy izzad kombinációja mogorvaság és vékonyan fátyolos ellenségeskedés.

★ I believe you when you say that every single part of a pig is edible but I just want an egg sandwich please.
Azt hiszem, amikor azt mondja, hogy minden egyes része, sertés ehető, de én csak azt szeretném egy tojásos szendvicset, kérjük.

★ Your country has been responsible for the dynamo, the ballpoint pen and Rubik's cube so why can't you invent a way for me to buy a railway ticket without having to queue for twenty-five minutes?
Az Ön országa volt felelős a dinamó, a golyóstoll és a Rubik-kocka, miért nem tudsz kitalálni a módját, hogy vegyek egy vasúti jegyet, anélkül, hogy sorban 25 percig?

ITALY

Italy is not technically part of the Third World,
but no one has told the Italians.
P. J. O'Rourke

MICHELANGELO, GUCCI, SPAGHETTI carbonara, the Cosa Nostra ... there are few places where art, fashion, carbohydrates and organised crime intermingle as effortlessly as in Italy. The Italians have a saying, 'la dolce vita', which means the sweet life; a life of pleasures and indulgences. Sure, on the face of it Italy *does* seem to have everything: a benign climate, a host of cultural treasures, well-dressed criminals, an edible national cuisine plus a reputation as a country that's stylish, elegant and chic.

Mention Italy and most people think of glamorous associations: Ferrari, Lamborghini, Martini, Prada, Bulgari, Armani ... the list of elite brands is endless (well, until you get down to Nutella and Ferrero Rocher), but scratch the surface and you'll find a country that's as superficial as its fashion industry.

Strip off Italy's clothes and you'll see a country in financial meltdown like all its southern European neighbours, slipping into recession quicker than a Naples pickpocket removing your wallet. This situation is exacerbated by the country's long history of political instability (more than twenty-five governments since 1980), a reputation for lumbering bureaucracy and a work ethic that makes the Spanish look like models of efficiency.

The persona Italy still keeps promoting to the world is Rudolph Valentino. The reality is that it's Joey Tribbiani from Friends.

FIVE ABSOLUTELY TRUE FACTS ABOUT ITALY
(NONE OF WHICH WILL INSPIRE YOU TO VISIT)·

* In a recent gender equality survey Italy ranked seventy-fourth in the world, one place behind Kazakhstan... and that's a country where women pull ploughs and mine bauxite.
* Italy suffers more earthquakes than any other European country; forty-four since the year 2000. As recently as 1980 a quake in Naples killed 3,000 people.
* Almost four-fifths of Italy is either mountainous or hilly.
* Italians are always bragging about their culinary history but conveniently forget that modern Italian cuisine is almost entirely a late nineteenth century fabrication (before then the staple diet was bread and olives). Three of the foods most associated with the country weren't even invented there; ice cream as we know it was invented by the Chinese about the middle of the seventh century, dried pasta was introduced by Arabs in the thirteenth century, while it's generally accepted that pizza was first cooked by the ancient Greeks or Egyptians.
* Soccer fans in Italy are called *tifosi*, which translates literally as 'carriers of typhoid'.

ROME

There's a saying, Rome wasn't built in day; well it's a pity it wasn't. Because they took so bloody long, the city is overrun with thousands of relics, statues and monuments, which means it's correspondingly overrun with hundreds of thousands of tourists gawping at them, blocking every single street and piazza.

The continual excavation work going on means you're not certain if you're visiting a huge museum or a demolition site. Turn a corner and there's a memorial to Augustus – or is it Tiberius? Who's that on that plinth? Antonio Pius or Lucius Verus? This relentless barrage of generic photo-fit emperors everywhere you go makes any trip to Rome repetitive and tiresome.

Rome is called the eternal city for a reason: even a long weekend drags on like a whole week.

Attractions to avoid

★ **Trevi Fountain (Fontana di Trevi)** The Paris Hilton of historic monuments, the Trevi Fountain is overrated, underwhelming and famous for being famous. Legend claims that whomever throws a coin into the waters will return to Rome. That is reason enough to ensure your money remains secure within your pockets, purse or wallet.

★ **The Colosseum** Also called the Flavian Amphitheatre, and a huge roundabout, this half demolished sports stadium is a focal point in Rome. For tourists it's also a focal point for irritating street vendors who'll chase you round and round the monument trying to sell anything from a plastic gladiator's helmet to a nodding Michelangelo's David.

★ **Spanish Steps (Piazza di Spagna)** The most interesting thing to say about steps is that you can walk up them and you can walk down them. The difference with the Spanish Steps is that you can't even do this easily as they are perpetually overrun by thousands of seated tourists who cover every single square inch. If you do eventually manage to reach the bottom you'll find a square with a dirty clogged fountain.

★ **Pantheon** A large restored Roman temple with a huge domed roof. That's it. There should be a policeman standing outside waving people away and saying, 'Move on. Nothing to see.'

Vatican City: the Catholic Disneyland

Although located within the city of Rome, the Vatican is actually an independent sovereign state – however, think of it as a sort of Catholic Disneyland, but far less organised and with far longer queues; there are the same high admission prices and expensive, vulgar gift shops but instead of looking out for Mickey on Main Street, people pack St Peter's Square for a glimpse of the Pope. Its main attractions include:

★ **Sistine Chapel:** Cattle being herded to a slaughterhouse enjoy better conditions – and are more satisfied with the outcome. After shuffling inch-by-inch through what seems like a sauna filled with renaissance art, dehydration and a strained neck are not compensated by the eventual view of Michelangelo's scenes from the Book of Genesis. In these paintings the face of God looks very angry. So will you be.

★ **St Peter's Basilica:** Reputedly one of the finest cathedrals in the world. Actually a disgusting show of opulence and wealth from a religion that preaches humility and simplicity.

★ **Vatican Museum:** Portraits, frescos and statues that all look the same in a museum with absolutely no understanding of the concept of 'directional signage'.

★ **The Swiss Guard:** This is the Vatican City's army, which eschews combat fatigues for the colourful costume of medieval jesters. The effectiveness of their pikestaffs (and, one assumes, Swiss Army Knives) against a terrorist attack is questionable.

Other places in Italy to avoid

★ **Pisa** The only city where subsidence is a tourist attraction.
★ **Pompeii** Guidebooks promise that Pompeii offers an amazing glimpse into the daily life of an average Roman town. What they don't say is that it also offers an amazing glimpse into how not to run a major

tourist attraction. The ruins are encrusted not just with 2000-year-old lava but also with cigarette butts and fast-food packaging. Visit here and you'll have to endure not just groups of annoying feral dogs that live among the ruins but groups of annoying feral-looking hawkers who'll pester you to buy poor, inadequate guided tours. Official notices that say 'Some buildings might be closed' confuse the word 'Some' for 'Nearly all' while food served in the café seems to have been originally prepared shortly before Vesuvius erupted.

★ **Tuscany** An area to the northwest of Italy, the capital of which is Florence, and best known for its rustic landscapes, olive groves and vineyards. During the summer months you might become irritated by high-pitched whining. However, this is not due to mosquitoes, but an infestation of really annoying British middle class families who look and sound exactly like David and Samantha Cameron.

★ **Turin** The northern industrial city of Turin is most famous for the Shroud of Turin, a centuries-old linen cloth that bears the image of Jesus Christ. Or it could be Edward I. Or Billy Connolly. To be honest, it's not that clear and, anyway, the Shroud is currently kept in the Royal Chapel of the Cathedral of St John the Baptist and is not on general display. So there.

★ **Venice** The Romans gave the world efficient drainage systems but visit Venice and it becomes apparent that they ran out of money and/or interest when they reached this northeastern coastal city. The Grand Canal smells like it's some sort of huge holding pool for all of the city's effluent while you'll notice a different type of aroma around St Mark's Square (Piazza San Marco); gaudy advertising banners, rip-off cafés and shoddy souvenirs fill this area with the stench of ugly commercialism.

★ **Sicily** Sicilians have a saying: 'When you discover Sicily you discover the world.' What they don't tell you is that they're referring to the world of organised crime, institutionalised corruption and people with middle names like 'the shark' and 'razors'. As the Mediterranean's largest island and an autonomous region of Italy, Sicily is proud of its differences from the mainland. Although Italy has more art masterpieces per square mile than anywhere else in the world, Sicily's claim to fame is that it has more people per square mile called Vito. Walk down any Sicilian street and it feels like you're on the set of the Godfather. Although the mafia is no longer the force it once was, there are still many people with links to the Cosa Nostra. To avoid trouble remember never to use the term 'Mafioso'. Instead use the locally accepted euphemism, 'Men of Honour'.

★ **Milan** Milan in the north has been described as a city obsessed with glamour and money, with locals who are conceited and pretentious. This is a place less concerned with its historic past than its reputation as fashion capital of the world and home to Italian celebrities; a city that reveres Paolo Maldini over Botticelli and Monica Belluci over Leonardo da Vinci. Ask a passer-by about 'The Last Supper' and they'll probably recommend any of the four Michelin starred restaurants rather than giving you directions to see the painting at the Monastery of Santa Maria delle Grazie.

THE ROME POLICE

Rome is a city where the police look like male models and where uniforms featuring brocade and sashes never went out of fashion. The overall impression, however, is that the police are just there for show, such is their apparent reluctance to enforce any degree of law and order. Rome is rife not just with relics but also petty criminals, pickpockets and annoying rat-faced vendors hawking knock-off watches and designer goods on every corner while police look the other way (usually to catch their reflection in a shop window).

DID YOU KNOW?

★ Most Italians drive on the right side of the road.

★ Benito Mussolini, Italy's wartime fascist leader, tried to eliminate foreign words from Italian, particularly the names of Disney characters. Donald Duck was renamed 'Paperino', Mickey Mouse became 'Topolino' and Goofy was known as 'Pippo'.

Five reasons you know you're in Italy

❶ **It's like being in a mime show** Most Italians can have an entire conversation that consists entirely of eye movements, facial expressions, shoulder shrugging and violent hand gestures. On some occasions they cannot speak without it looking like they are conducting an orchestra.

❷ **And when they do talk, all conversations sound like ferocious arguments** Don't worry. The man and woman who look like they're having a blazing stand-up row in the street are just talking about the weather.

❸ **You'll end your visit in the Italian version of A & E** Italians are proud of their ability to multi-task. Unfortunately for pedestrians this specifically applies to Italian motorists who think nothing of overtaking, using the phone, reading a map, reading the paper, lighting a cigarette, drinking coffee, turning to speak to the passengers in the back and cursing the mothers or sisters of fellow motorists – simultaneously.

❹ **Every street feels like the catwalk** Walk down the road and it'll feel like everyone's judging your fashion sense. That's because they are. Brought up in a culture where's there's only two seasons (spring/summer and autumn/winter) and where some of the first words learned include *cuciture a contrasto* (contrasting stitching), everyone is ultra-conscious about appearances. They call themselves fashionistas. You'll call them shallow twats.

⑤ **You'll do more shopping than you intended** Spend time in most Italian towns or cities and two things are likely to get pinched; your bottom or your handbag.

USEFUL PHRASES TO USE IN ITALY

★ Your olive skin, luxuriant chest hair and tight, well-tailored trousers do not give you the automatic right to start hitting on my wife.
La tua pelle olivastra, capelli petto rigoglioso e ben stretti, pantaloni su misura non ti danno il diritto automatico ad iniziare sedurre mia moglie.

★ I have been waiting for ninety minutes. I had no idea that your advertised opening times were indicative only.
Ho aspettato per novanta minuti. Non avevo idea che i vostri orari di apertura sono stati annunciati solo indicativi.

★ I am very sorry. I didn't realise that the swarthy man I've just been talking to was actually your elderly mother.
Mi dispiace molto. Non mi rendevo conto che l'uomo dalla carnagione scura che ho appena parlato era in realtà, tua madre anziana.

PEOPLE SAY THE NICEST THINGS ABOUT ITALY . . .

Anarchy tempered by bureaucracy.
George F. Will

Italians are Frenchmen in a good mood.
Jean Cocteau

Italy is the paradise of the flesh, the hell of the soul, the purgatory of the pocketbook.
German saying

Venice is excessively ugly in the rain – it looks like King's Cross.
Sir John Gielgud

If there is a Hell, Rome is built on top of it.
German saying

Venice is like eating an entire box of chocolate liqueurs at one go.
Truman Capote

Italy is a paradise for horses and hell for women.
German saying

Italian devotion and German fasting have no meaning.
Danish saying

Half an Italian in a house is one too many.
German and French saying

Italian soup.
Czech term for poison

The Italian will kill his father for money.
Greek saying

To cook an egg, to make a bed for a dog and to teach an Italian to do anything are three hard things.
German saying

Italy is a paradise inhabited by devils.
German saying

An ass in Germany is a professor in Rome.
German saying

Genoa has mountains without wood, sea without fish,
women without shame and men without conscience.
English saying

Italy is a paradise inhabited by devils.
German saying

LATVIA

It's where Romanians go to feel better about themselves.

Anonymous

THE BALTIC STATE of Latvia is often described as being 'undiscovered' by tourists. This is not strictly true. Tourists definitely know all about it, it's just that they choose to avoid it like the plague (apart from as a stag weekend venue – see below – in which case you're likely to catch a dose of the plague).

'A country still in transition' is the euphemism used to describe day-to-day living after Latvia's independence from Russia in 1991. What this means is a country where you see BMWs driving past neglected, decaying public buildings, old women sweeping the streets in the shadows of billboards advertising 50-inch plasma TVs – and where roller-ball pens and bananas are still luxury items.

When it comes to museums there are several where you can learn about the country's history under oppressive Nazi and Soviet occupations. Those who prefer farm machinery to massacres are also well-catered for; make sure you leave enough time to visit the Museum of Agriculture Machinery.

To be frank, although there's not a whole lot of interesting things to do in Latvia, the saving grace is that you get round the whole place quickly. This fact has been recognised by the Latvian Tourism

Development Agency, which actually boasts that for travellers 'the best thing about Latvia is that it is so compact'.

Arrive and expect little and you won't be disappointed.

RIGA

The capital city of Latvia is often described as the gem of the Baltics. However, this is rather like saying that Croydon is the gem of the south east London/Surrey borders. Despite the city's best attempts to present itself as a focal point of historic architecture Riga today is far better known for its reputation as one of the cheapest stag trip destinations, a situation which the authorities desperately try to play down. Riga has been described by numerous travel writers as a city that 'gets under your skin'. After experiencing some of the stag trip entertainment this description can be taken quite literally.

What the Riga Tourist Development Agency want you to remember after visiting their city	What you'll actually remember after experiencing Riga's reputation for cheap stag weekends
Stunning Riga Castle, which dates back to 1440	An abundance of lonely looking women with low self-esteem and badly applied make-up
The unusual wooden architecture of Kalnciema Street	Being offered a blowie and a hamburger for less than a fiver
The imposing Stalinesque architecture of the Latvian Academy of Sciences	Novelty acts that makes the Thai ping pong trick look positively mundane
The Central Market, Europe's largest market and bazaar	Seeing a girl and a donkey engaged in sexual congress on stage
The beautiful thirteenth-century Dome Cathedral	A happy ending

Attractions to avoid

★ **Riga Central Market** If you fancy a plate of smoked eels and beetroot, pastries with fillings that defy identification, copper and amber Baltic 'jewellery' or tasteless knitwear that wouldn't look out of place on someone in an eHarmony advertisement, then make sure you visit the Central Market.

   Visited by up to 100,000 people a day, this huge historic market enjoys all the ambience of a group of Zeppelin hangars – mainly as it's partially housed within these structures. Heralded as the largest market in Europe it offers, in the words of the official Latvian Tourism Development Agency, 'almost everything'. What it doesn't offer is anything you actually want.

★ **The House of Blackheads** One of the biggest tourist attractions in Riga's old town. I'm not sure what this is and, quite frankly, I feel ill just contemplating it.

FIVE ABSOLUTELY TRUE FACTS ABOUT LATVIA
(NONE OF WHICH WILL INSPIRE YOU TO VISIT)

★ The Jurmala Open Air Museum has the largest collection of ropes in Latvia.

★ The world's fourth largest church organ can be found in the Dome Cathedral.

★ Riga is the only city in the world that celebrates Sherlock Holmes' birthday.

★ Latvia boasts one of the highest male suicide rates in the world.

★ *Kvass* is a locally produced drink made from the natural fermentation of rye bread. Coca Cola are not unduly concerned.

Useful Latvian phrases

⭐ I did not mean to call your country 'Little Russia'. Please stop punching me in the stomach.

Es negribēju, lai izsauktu jūsu valsts 'Little Krieviju'. Lūdzu pārtraukt caurumošanas mani kuņģī.

⭐ Taxi driver, are you sure your short-cut down this one-way street at 110 kph is safe? And please stop reading the map while you are driving.

Taksometra vadītājs, jūs esat pārliecināts, ka jūsu īstermiņa samazināt šo vienvirziena iela 110 KPH ir droša? Un, lūdzu, pārtrauciet lasot karti, kamēr Jūs vadītāja.

⭐ My penis has turned green after a stag weekend. Do you sell an appropriate ointment?

Mans penis ir kļuvusi zaļa pēc briedis weekend. Vai jūs pārdodat atbilstošu ziede?

Five reasons you know you're in Latvia

① **Taxi drivers who settle discussions over fares with knives** An abundance of unscrupulous taxi drivers charge fares based more on a whim than a meter and will often add a range of 'extras' when you arrive at your destination. Taking rides in these cabs will leave you ripped off and/or ripped open.

② **There's always someone willing to pick a fight with you** Rampant alcoholism and a culture that equates heavy drinking with machismo mean it's very easy for visitors to get into trouble. In order to stay out of trouble it's best to have knowledge of basic Latvian and mixed martial arts.

③ **You're involved in a road traffic accident within minutes of leaving the airport** With driving skills learned from watching a pirate DVD of

The Fast and the Furious and a devil-may-care attitude towards road signs, speed limits and pedestrians it's not surprising that Latvian drivers have one of the highest accident rates in the west.

❹ **Racial attitudes stuck in the 1950s** If you're non-white and walk down a busy street, expect locals to dash out of pubs and bars as you walk by. This is not out of any form of inquisitiveness, but because they want to make sure you clearly hear the racial abuse they're yelling.

❺ **Two-tier pricing** When ordering drinks expect to be charged three or four times what the locals pay. Don't cause a scene with the barman unless you feel like discussing this inequality with a burly member of the Russian Mafia, which has a vested interest in most bars and clubs.

LITHUANIA

The Lithuanian is stupid like a pig but cunning like a serpent.
Polish saying

THE SMALL EAST European country of Lithuania is often described as 'the Spain of the Baltics'. This is complimentary only if you want your country to be associated with bad food, laziness as a national trait and 26% unemployment. It's also been described as 'rebellious, quirky and unpredictable' but that sounds like you're visiting Lindsay Lohan rather than one of the poorest, most backward nations in the EU.

Saying that a trip to Lithuania will be an unpleasant experience is like saying Bill Gates is wealthy. However, despite this reputation, tourism is on the rise; the problem is, so is neo-Nazism. Spend time in the capital Vilnius on Independence Day and you can experience both the colourful May Day parade and a march of 1,000 neo-Nazis. Lithuania is a country apparently proud of its racism and has actually devised its own 'designer version' of the swastika. If that wasn't objectionable enough, in May 2010 a local court in the western city of Klaipeda ruled that swastikas were part of 'Lithuania's historical heritage rather than symbols of Nazi Germany'.

If you do visit Lithuania ensure you take out the maximum travel insurance possible. According to the EU's official statistics agency

Eurostat, you're more likely to be murdered in Lithuania than anywhere else in the EU.

Happy holidays.

KNOW YOUR EUPHEMISMS: A GUIDE TO SURVIVING LITHUANIA

What they say	What they mean
★ Frozen in time	★ Dilapidated
★ Unspoilt	★ Squalid
★ Refreshingly unpretentious	★ Primitive
★ Old world charm	★ Uncivilised
★ Friendly locals	★ Beggars

VILNIUS

The capital of Lithuania, located in the south east of the country was voted European City of Culture in 2009. This is widely believed to have been the result of a counting error or a pity vote. Just as patriotism is the last refuge of a scoundrel, 'an abundance of baroque architecture' is the last refuge of a capital city trying to make itself sound vaguely interesting. Note to the Vilnius Tourist Office: a cobbled old town is not a sufficient reason to visit your capital.

LITHUANIAN CUISINE: YOUR FIVE A DAY

★ Grease
★ Excess of salt
★ Potatoes
★ More potatoes
★ Yet more potatoes

DID YOU KNOW?

⭐ It's been claimed that Lithuanians reserve a special hatred for the Greeks for inventing the word xenophobia before they had a chance.

Some attractions to avoid

⭐ **The Gate of Dawn** A chapel built above a sixteenth-century city fortification; now one of Eastern Europe's leading pilgrimage destinations. Believers come here to ask the black Virgin Mary icon to grant their wishes, most of which are understood to be 'Get me home'.

⭐ **Užupis** Several well-respected guidebooks suggest tourists cross the Vilnia River to watch the drunks of Užupis, an unofficial breakaway state from Lithuania. When a list of a country's attractions involves watching alcoholics, you know you're scrapping the very bottom of the sightseeing barrel.

FIVE ABSOLUTELY TRUE FACTS ABOUT LITHUANIA
(NONE OF WHICH WILL INSPIRE YOU TO VISIT)

⭐ It features the world's only statue of Frank Zappa.

⭐ Say bye-bye to bunny; Lithuanian children receive their eggs from the Easter Granny.

⭐ Lithuanians believe that at midnight on Christmas Eve, animals can talk.

⭐ Don't get married here if you want a toaster or set of saucepans; the traditional Lithuanian wedding gift is a loaf of bread and some salt.

⭐ Vilnius.life.com states that the country's annual 'Physics Day' hosted by the physics department of Vilnius University is 'one of the most outlandish days' in the city's events calendar.

Five reasons you know you're in Lithuania

❶ **An abundance of right-wing skinheads** They call themselves patriots. Most others call them Nazi scum. The police have a soft spot for them.

❷ **One of the rarest phrases you'll hear is 'thank you'** Lithuanians have a reputation for rudeness to foreigners and make it clear you're unwelcome. It's said they have one word for 'Hello' and forty words for 'fuck off'.

❸ **You'll be bothered by a beggar every thirty paces (ten in the cities)** It's like being in a country where 60% of the country are *Big Issue* sellers who happen to be handy with a knife.

❹ **If you speak any language other than Lithuanian or Russian there's a likelihood someone will spit at you.** Many Lithuanians confuse the concept of national pride with that of violent prejudice (see point 1).

❺ **1960s standards of technology** Ask if a café has wifi and you'll be laughed at; that or burned as a witch.

Useful Lithuanian phrases

★ I requested a glass of beer not lukewarm dishwater.
Aš paprašė bokalą alaus. Aš nenoriu drungno pamazgos.

★ I assure you that I love Hitler. Now will you please stop jumping on my head?
Aš užtikrinu jus, kad aš myliu Hitlerį. Dabar jūs nustokite šokinėja ant mano galvos?

★ Is there something interesting to do that doesn't involve baroque architecture?
Ar kažką įdomaus padaryti, kad nėra susijusi su baroko architektūros?

LUXEMBOURG

On a clear day, from the terrace … you can't see Luxembourg at all.
This is because a tree is in the way.

Alan Coren

AS A COUNTRY, Luxembourg is like one of those completely anonymous kids who sit at the back of the classroom who no one really knows or cares about. Faceless and completely unremarkable, they have to join a whole raft of societies and organisations in order to make friends. In the case of Luxembourg these clubs have been the Belgium–Luxembourg Economic Union, the Western European Union, Benelux, NATO, the United Nations and, of course, the EU.

Ironically, Luxembourg's biggest claim to fame is its small size; it's the smallest landlocked country in the EU. With an area of less than 1,000 square miles it's difficult to take Luxembourg seriously as a sovereign state. It more accurately resembles an extension of its neighbours; think of it as France's conservatory, Germany's shed or Belgium's carport. Although the country can be traced back to 963 AD, up until relatively recently other nations refused to believe it actually existed, mistaking its presence on the map for a small stain or a printing error.

If, for any reason, you are considering visiting Luxembourg take heed of an actual proverb from the country which translates as, 'Each of us has but one life so why waste it in Luxembourg?'

DID YOU KNOW?

★ The country's official title is the Grand Duchy of Luxembourg. This ridiculous self-aggrandisement can be compared to saying, 'The Magnificent State of Eritrea' or 'The Glorious Kingdom of Canvey Island'.

★ A native of Luxembourg is called a Luxembourger, which sounds less like a nationality and more like something very small, bland and unsatisfying you'd find in one of the country's McDonald's.

LUXEMBOURG CITY

With a name as unimaginative as most of its population, the capital combines the worst of both worlds: city prices with a provincial mentality.

Attractions to avoid

★ **Notre Dame Cathedral (Cathedrale Notre Dame)** Be warned! This seventeenth-century cathedral built in the Gothic style is not THE Notre Dame. It was built to attract gullible tourists or those who confuse the words 'Paris' with 'Luxembourg City'.

★ **Luxembourg Casino** Go here expecting buzz, excitement and the chance to win back some of the money you've wasted on your trip up until now and you'll be sorely disappointed. This misleadingly named attraction is actually a poorly maintained art museum. The odds of enjoying yourself here are stacked against you.

★ **Utopolis Luxembourg** You know there's not much to see or do in the capital when a large multiplex cinema is listed as a main attraction. Worth a visit if you like sticky carpets, popcorn the same price as a gourmet meal for two or the latest Adam Sandler masterpiece in Dutch with Belgian subtitles.

FIVE ABSOLUTELY TRUE FACTS ABOUT LUXEMBOURG
(NONE OF WHICH WILL INSPIRE YOU TO VISIT)

★ The last important visitor to Luxembourg was author Victor Hugo, who stayed there back in 1871.

★ Luxembourgers are not without irony. In 1886 industrialist Henri Owen Tudor developed the first practical lead-acid battery in the world. He later died from lead poisoning.

★ The country's most famous artist was Joseph Jean Ferdinand Kutter, who painted his subjects with excessively large noses. Kutter polarised critics who claimed his portraits demonstrated either a 'radical form of expressionism' or were 'the work of an imbecile'.

★ Those who claim Luxembourg has contributed nothing to world culture should remember that RTL, the country's entertainment group, is responsible for both The X-Factor and Pop Idol.

★ It is compulsory to have windscreen wipers fitted to your car, but you don't need an actual windscreen.

Five reasons you know you're in Luxembourg

❶ **It has one of the highest percentages of mobile phones per head in Europe** Which also means it has, pro rata, the highest number of annoying Black Eyed Peas ringtones.

❷ **There are over 150 different banks in the country** This is good as it means you're never far from an ATM, but bad as you're likely to be stuck behind a North Korean despot trying to make a withdrawal (in September 2010 it was reported that Kim Jong-il of North Korea held $4bn in secret accounts in Luxembourg banks).

❸ **Luxembourgers confuse the word 'famous' with 'inconsequential'** According to one completely un-ironic website, the most celebrated Luxembourgers include Jonas Ferdinand Gabriel Lippmann, inventor of the first capillary electrometer and Georges Christen, the first man to inflate hot water bottles just by lung power.

❹ **There is no overwhelming sense of ambition, pride or drive for self-improvement** This may not be that surprising when you consider the official motto of Luxembourg is 'Mir wëlle bleiwe wat mir sinn', which translates as, 'We want to remain what we are'.

❺ **Everyone looks disorientated** No one ever goes to Luxembourg on purpose. They usually end up there as a result of accidentally crossing a border when it's dark or foggy, or being deposited there, naked and drunk, as part of a stag night prank.

USEFUL PHRASES TO USE IN LUXEMBOURG

★ I do not use your country as a tax haven so what makes you think you are justified in charging me twelve euros for this small cup of coffee?
Je n'utilise pas votre pays comme un paradis fiscal, si c'est ce qui vous fait penser qu'il est justifié de me demander douze euros pour cette petite tasse de café?

★ Can you tell me where I can find a visitor attraction that is vaguely interesting or at least remotely tolerable?
Pouvez-vous me dire où je peux trouver une attraction touristique qui soit vaguement intéressante ou au moins à une distance acceptable?

★ I can't believe Luxembourg City was named European Capital of Culture twice. I can only put this down to some sort of gross miscount or election fraud.
Je ne peux pas croire Luxembourg a été nommée capitale européenne de la culture deux fois. Je ne peux que mettre cela sur le compte d'une erreur grave ou d'une fraude électorale.

MALTA

There's one reason young Maltese men wear moustaches;
it's so they can look like their mothers.

Anonymous

THE MEDITERRANEAN ISLAND of Malta (just 122 square miles in area) proves beyond any doubt that good things do not come in small packages.

Its strategic location has meant that during its colourful history Malta was constantly visited by explorers and invaders from Europe and North Africa; Phoenicians, Greeks, Carthaginians, Romans, Moors, Normans, Castilians, Habsburgs and Turks. The fact that none chose to settle there must say something about Malta. Even the Knights of the Order of St John, who were given the Island in 1530, couldn't bear the place. So desperate were they to leave that in 1798 they actually surrendered to Napoleon without a fight.

So what is the appeal of this insignificant country? Malta's warm climate and coastline have made it a package holiday destination for those who left it too late to book into the Costa del Sol, the Canaries or Majorca. Malta tries to compensate for the fact that it's the third or fourth choice by positioning itself as a more sophisticated destination. Proof of this, they claim, is that the holiday entertainment is a cut above the rest. However even this is questionable when you consider these 'top international acts' include an ex-Blackpool pier comedian, a Greek puppeteer and the Serbian version of Peters and Lee.

The country has worked hard to provide visitor attractions that are on a par with the best of a tired British seaside town, while tourist amenities can match anything that the Democratic Republic of the Congo can offer.

What Malta lacks in things to do, it more than makes up for in mediocrity.

Five absolutely true facts about Malta
(none of which will inspire you to visit)

★ The national dish is fenkata, which sounds exotic until you learn that it's a communal meal of rabbit stew (you can find live rabbits sold for food in many street markets).

★ If you're female, over twenty-one and unmarried, the locals will automatically think you're a lesbian.

★ Musician Robert Palmer was raised in Malta (and the Maltese will never ever let you forget that).

★ You could visit a different church every day of the year and still not have time to see them all.

★ Most of the shoreline is rocky and there are hardly any sandy beaches.

Valletta: Church capital of the world

If you like churches, you'll love Valletta. Despite having an area of less than one-third of a square mile, the capital of Malta is crammed with no less than twenty-four churches and one cathedral. The only other place of note here is the Grandmaster's Palace. Visitors hoping to see the crib of one of the pioneers of hip-hop, DJing and mixing, will be very disappointed since this oddly-named building is just the seat of the Maltese Parliament.

Mdina: Second church capital of the world

The old fortified city features another cathedral and more churches, grottos and crypts. Visit the underground catacombs that boast a series of Byzantine frescos. Then again, don't.

MALTESE WINE

A label proclaiming 'Wine made in Malta' should be taken as a warning or at least as confirmation that you have indeed purchased a bottle of vinegar or drain cleaner. While some Maltese reds can be compared to the best Angolan whites, many are described graciously as 'an acquired taste', 'different', or by the less charitable 'deeply disturbing'. Many Maltese wines can be identified by a number of common characteristics: a bouquet of burning tyres, the flavour of antiseptic mouthwash and the aftertaste of cough linctus.

Five reasons you know you're in Malta

❶ **You get the impression that the Second World War has only just ended**
An abundance of rubble, derelict buildings and damaged roads give the impression that the intensive German and Italian bombing of Malta finished in 2012 rather than in 1942.

❷ **The streets are covered in dead mice, litter and dog poo** Maltese street cleaners display a southern European attitude to the work ethic. And hygiene.

❸ **You find yourself walking in single file** Narrow pavements make it impossible to overtake the endless procession of white-haired Maltese widows you'll always find in front of you.

❹ **You find religion after a bus ride** It is impossible for Maltese bus drivers to negotiate the island's many treacherous hairpin bends at breakneck speed without talking on a mobile phone or turning round and chatting to friends seated behind them.

❺ **A total ignorance of the term 'value for money'** Since joining the EU in 2004 restaurant prices have increased significantly, a combination of inflation and pure, unadulterated greed.

MALTA: THE NEW MOSQUITO COAST

Malta welcomed a new breed of international traveller in 2010; the Asian tiger mosquito. The insect can be found all over the island and unlike regular mosquitoes, is also very active during daytime. Official guidance to tourists includes wearing 'socks, shoes, long trousers and long-sleeved shirts when outdoors'. Useful advice when the country promotes itself as a summer holiday destination.

Useful Maltese phrases

★ Mr Hotelier, you have obviously confused the term '5 star' with '2 star'.
Mr lukandier, inti ovvjament konfuż it-terminu '5 stilel' ma '2 stilel'.

★ Is that another historic ruin or just another half-built apartment block?
Hija li ieħor rovina storiku jew biss ieħor blokk appartamenti nofs mibnija?

★ Can I please purchase a gallon of mosquito repellent?
Nista jekk jogħġbok jixtri gallun ta 'nemus ripellant?

THE NETHERLANDS

Dutch is not so much a language as a disease of the throat.
Mark Twain

THE NETHERLANDS (or Holland as it's sometimes known, probably so the country can receive a double EU farming subsidy) has a reputation for a liberal attitude towards sex, drugs and ridiculous footwear, which is why the country can be summed up in just three words: prostitution, cannabis and clogs.

Foreign visitors can find the country's broadminded outlook both extremely bewildering or remarkably engaging, depending on whether they're visiting the country to enjoy its historical landmarks or just to smoke weed and have intercourse.

The country has also had a long reputation for encouraging the arts and you'll find a multitude of well-respected museums in its main cities. However, before you spend money visiting them, just remember that the country responsible for Rembrandt, Vermeer and van Gogh then went on to invent *Big Brother*.

But even this pales into insignificance when you consider that even bigger abomination unleashed on the world, the oxymoron Dutch cuisine. Spend time in the Netherlands and you'll soon discover that the Dutch are to food what Vin Diesel is to Oscar nominations. Almost universally decried as bland and tasteless, it will come as no surprise to learn that Australian soldiers serving with Dutch troops in Afghanistan rejected outright the food prepared by their allies. And when Australians, among the most undiscerning foodies in the world, complain about the quality of meals, you know you're in trouble.

If you must visit the Netherlands, eat before you go.

THE RED-LIGHT DISTRICT

For many, this is the sole reason for visiting Amsterdam. The area is promoted by the Netherlands Board of Tourism as one of the oldest and most beautiful parts of the city, with winding, narrow, cobbled streets and charming fourteenth-century architecture where beautiful women parade their wares in red-fringed window parlours. The reality, however, is somewhat different.

The district is indeed filled with narrow, cobbled streets but these in turn are filled with giggling Japanese tourists, annoying American frat boys and seedy sex shops selling magazines called *Donkey Stonk*. And while some of the women are indeed beautiful (in a damaged sort of way) most look like sad-eyed housewives whose lives are heavy with regret and who would enter into sex with as much enthusiasm as a Dutchman taking part in Masterchef.

NB Rim City (Randstad) is the name given to Amsterdam's heavily developed western sector. It is not part of the Red-Light District.

AMSTERDAM

In the 1960s the capital of the Netherlands was seen as a utopian dream a place where people believed anything could happen; they were wrong. Amsterdam has always been dull. It's said that Anne Frank hid in her attic to escape the Nazis. The truth was that it was more interesting than going outside.

HAARLEM VS HARLEM

Haarlem, a city about 12 miles west of Amsterdam, has absolutely nothing in common with its namesake, Harlem in New York City. This is how you can tell the difference:

Haarlem, The Netherlands	Harlem, New York
What you can buy on the street	
Twenty-eight types of cheese	Twenty-eight types of hard drugs
Most popular art movement	
Dutch Golden Age	Spray-painted squiggles
Footwear of choice	
Gaily painted clogs	$250 Air Jordans
Favourite son	
Frans Hals	Ghostface Killa
Flowers of choice	
Tulips	What motherf*ckin' flowers!

Attractions to avoid

★ **Dam Square** Once the historical centre of the city and its ancient marketplace, Dam Square is better known today for an infestation of pigeons and street entertainers. If you enjoy being shat on or watching people walking against the wind, painted silver and sitting motionless for the entire day, or playing excruciatingly badly to a Kenny G backing track, then this is a must-see.

★ **The canals** Due to the multitude of canals that wind their way through the city centre, Amsterdam is often called the Venice of the North – but then again, so is Birmingham. Most of the canal boat trips promise visitors an 'unforgettable experience'. This is true since you'll hear an intelligible commentary over the din of noisy boat engines and windows that look like they haven't been cleaned since the Franco-Dutch war.

★ **The Heineken Experience** Come here if you've ever wanted to see old fermentation tanks plus endless coasters, bottles and beer steins from Heineken's rich heritage. It isn't even a real working brewery; that closed and was moved from the site in 1988. Not so much an experience as a corporate brainwashing event.

★ **Reypenaer Cheese Tasting Rooms** Visitors suffer a video covering every aspect of cheese production and then have an opportunity to try six different cheeses, or are they soaps? Some people claim it's difficult to distinguish between the two. Not recommended for those who display any intolerance to milk-based foods (or appalling tourist attractions).

ALL ABOUT WINDMILLS AND TULIPS

★ There's absolutely nothing of interest to say about these.

ROTTERDAM

The Netherlands' second largest city, which has a long-standing rivalry with Amsterdam. There are many stories of how each city has tried to out-do the other throughout their long histories but, to be honest, these are incredibly dull and not worth recounting.

DID YOU KNOW?

★ The Dutch traditionally only eat one hot meal a day (and the term 'meal' is used loosely).

★ It's been said that Dutch sounds like a German with a throat full of phlegm trying to speak Welsh (hence the term 'phlegmish').

★ **Euromast Tower** Rotterdam's version of getting high; you can ascend this 328-foot tower to get 360-degree views across the city and harbour to the soundtrack of 'Space Oddity' by David Bowie. More appropriate music would be 'Bored Out Of My Mind' by The Manic Street Preachers.

★ **FutureLand Maasvlakte 2** One of the very best places in the whole of the Netherlands to learn all about dredging and how the Dutch reclaimed land from the sea.

FIVE ABSOLUTELY TRUE FACTS ABOUT THE NETHERLANDS
(NONE OF WHICH WILL INSPIRE YOU TO VISIT)

★ The Dutch biosphere contains the highest levels of acid, nitrates and phosphate.

★ Google 'beautiful dikes in Holland' and you'll get disappointing information about flood control and levee systems.

★ Not all of the women you see sitting in the windows in the Red-Light District are really women.

★ It's normal to eat toast covered in chocolate sprinkles and sausages (frikadel) made from offal; anything from brain to intestines.

★ There are more bicycles than members of the population.

Five reasons you know you're in the Netherlands

❶ **You can't walk down a street without bumping into someone** Holland is the most densely populated country in Europe, which means 'love thy neighbour' isn't just an adage, it's a necessity. This, however, can cause problems when your neighbour happens to be a prostitute.

❷ **All the locals are very welcoming, laid back and friendly** The Dutch government decriminalised cannabis in 1976. That's the reason.

❸ **People will be extra welcoming if you're ginger** Orange is the official colour of the Netherlands and a sign of patriotism.

❹ **The sauce served with your chips is very unlikely to be tomato ketchup** Although mayonnaise is the standard Dutch topping for chips you'll probably find yourself also being offered fries with peanut sauce (*friet met satésaus*) or fries with peanut sauce, mayonnaise and raw chopped onions (*patatje oorlog*).

❺ **You won't see eye to eye with many people** Statistically, the tallest people in the world are the Dutch. The average height for all adults is 6 feet 1 inch, which means you'll have an inferiority complex as soon as you arrive.

Useful Dutch phrases

★ No cannabis for me please. Just a skinny cappuccino.
Geen cannabis voor mij te behagen. Gewoon een magere cappuccino.

★ I had no idea you were born a man! Please refund me my money and do not tell my friends waiting outside.
Ik had geen idee dat je geboren een man! Gelieve terug te betalen me mijn geld en niet vertel mijn vrienden wachten buiten.

★ I know euthanasia is legal here but I am only suffering from a bad cold. Please take that syringe away from me!
Ik weet dat euthanasie is hier legaal, maar ik ben alleen maar last van een zware verkoudheid. Gelieve weg te nemen dat de spuit van mij!

ODE TO JOY: THE EUROPEAN ANTHEM: ALTERNATIVE (AND FAR MORE APPROPRIATE) SUGGESTIONS

YOU MIGHT NOT know, let alone even care, but since 1985 there's been a European anthem, chosen to express the ideals of 'freedom, peace and solidarity'.

It's called 'Ode to Joy' and is based on the final movement of Beethoven's Ninth Symphony. To be honest, it's not that memorable and sounds more like the background music from a commercial promoting health insurance, funeral services or the Third Reich, rather than something you'd want to hear on official occasions – if at all.

Having a European anthem called 'Ode to Joy' without any sense of irony is completely inappropriate. What we need is a new anthem with a title that sums up exactly what the EU represents or what people think of it. Suggestions include:

- 'Won't Get Fooled Again' – The Who
- 'Lies Greed Misery' – Linkin Park
- 'What a Waste' – Ian Dury and the Blockheads
- 'We Gotta Get Out of This Place' – The Animals
- 'Union of the Snake' – Duran Duran
- 'Badlands' – Bruce Springsteen
- 'Evil Ways' – Santana
- 'I Hate Everything About You' – Three Day's Grace
- 'Viva Hate' – Morrissey
- 'Ball of Confusion' – Temptations
- 'Lying Again' – Lynsey de Paul
- 'We Don't Care' – Demon Hunter

* ★ 'Simply Unstoppable' – Tinie Tempah
* ★ 'Shades of Grey' – Delilah
* ★ 'Livin' in a World Corrupt' – K-OS
* ★ 'Kill the President' – The Offspring
* ★ 'Money for Nothing' – Dire Straits
* ★ 'Welcome to the Machine' – Pink Floyd
* ★ 'Welcome to Hell' – Venom
* ★ 'Leave in Silence' – Depeche Mode
* ★ 'Bleeding Me' – Metallica
* ★ 'Supermassive Black Hole' – Muse

EUROPEAN OXYMORONS

Twenty-six phrases you'll never, ever hear used ...

* Austrian liberalism
* Belgian hysteria
* Bulgarian splendour
* Croatian sophistication
* Cypriot prosperity
* Czech craftsmanship
* Danish mountains
* Dutch cuisine
* Estonian charm
* Finnish extravagance
* French manners
* German levity
* Greek prudence

* Hungarian refinement
* Italian organisation
* Latvian style
* Lithuanian tolerance
* Luxembourg impulsiveness
* Maltese sophistication
* Polish glamour
* Portuguese productivity
* Romanian fashion
* Slovakian hospitality
* Slovenian elegance
* Spanish efficiency
* Swedish aggressiveness

POLAND

In the past few centuries, Poland has become known
as 'the airplane lavatory of Europe' – dirty, subject to turbulence,
and almost constantly occupied.
Chris Harris

THE LAST MAJOR influx of visitors to Poland took place in
September 1939 and it's not hard to see why. An average annual
temperature of just 6°C (falling to as little as −35°C in the
winter), an average 600 mm of rainfall and a strong chance of snow
from November to March make visitors cold and wet for a large part
of the year.

Then there's the general perception of the country itself. Ask most
people what words or phrases they associate with Poland and they'll often
say gloomy, religiously intolerant, archaic, bureaucratic, racially
prejudiced, backward, dishonest, hardship, dreary, sad and tragic. They
are, of course, correct. Add to this a surfeit of bad pickled food and an
infrastructure redolent of 1970s Britain and you won't want to kiss the
ground when you land there so much as slash your wrists.

So why go to Poland at all? The official tourist agency is keen to
promote the country's 'ever present sense of rich history'. This is true,
except that for rich, read 'sad or shameful', e.g. rife anti-Semitism,
German and Soviet invasions, Nazi death camps, the formation of
ghettos, collaboration with the enemy … All of these weigh heavily on
the Polish psyche so it's not surprising that many inhabitants have turned

to 40% vodka to help them deal with their dark past. You too may wish to rely on binge drinking to help you cope with your depressing visit.

WARSAW

The *Zycie Warszawy* (*Warsaw Life*) newspaper recently reported on a poll among European travellers that Warsaw was one of the most boring capitals in Europe, stating that the city was considered dull with nothing to offer. That is evidently not true as the capital of Poland can offer the tourist expanses of concrete, melancholy locals, ugly Soviet-era monuments and disappointment. They say a person who is tired of London is tired of life. Similarly, a person who is satisfied in Warsaw is a person with incredibly low expectations.

Attractions to avoid

★ **Old Town** When the Germans left Warsaw at the end of the Second World War they left the city a legacy of their occupation: the systematic and complete destruction of the Old Town. In a project that continued into the 1980s, the cobbled streets, baroque palaces, numerous churches and tiered burghers' houses were totally reconstructed. However, rather than just stop there, the authorities also took the opportunity to improve on the town square by ensuring there is now a sufficient number of tacky souvenir shops and expensive restaurants.

★ **New World Street (Nowy Swiat)** This mile-long historic boulevard is a main shopping street. Here you can buy the same brands you can find at home but with less choice and highly inflated prices. Think of it as the Oxford Street of Warsaw, offering the same degree of allure and class.

★ **Copernicus Science Centre** Forget the 450 interactive exhibits; this science museum that stands on the bank of the Vistula River is far better known for inconceivable levels of ineptitude and woefully insufficient staffing. Expect to queue for two to four hours just to gain admission, only to find yourself shuffling about in dangerously overcrowded conditions. The management here is oblivious to the concept of timed entry, pre-paid tickets or, indeed, any sense of organisation whatsoever. Creating a visitor-friendly attraction is not rocket science …

★ **Gestapo Headquarters Museum** Given the country's right-wing leanings it's unclear whether this attraction is a grim reminder of the horrors of Nazi occupation or a shrine to one of the most brutal secret police forces.

DID YOU KNOW?

★ When it comes to naming their dogs, the Poles are not very imaginative. The most popular name is Burek, which translates as 'brownish-grey colour'.

★ So many people fear or dislike Poland that the term Polonophobia needed to be invented.

KRAKOW

Krakow, Poland's second largest city, promotes itself as a city forged in battle, war, conquest and fate. This dramatic description conceals the fact that it's just another thirteenth-century merchants' town infested by tourists and local touts who prey on tourists. Making any eye contact whatsoever with the locals will result in you being greeted with 'You English? I have cousin who go to Manchester University. You know him?' and being offered fake designer watches and sunglasses, vouchers for disappointing city tours or coupons for free drinks at bars and clubs located down dodgy-looking medieval alleyways. Krakow is said to be Poland's trump card in the tourism stakes. It would be more accurate to call it the joker.

Attractions to avoid

★ **Main Market Square (Rynek Glowny)** Having the largest historic market square in Europe (it's spread across ten acres) is not necessarily something to boast about as it just means there's even more medieval palaces, churches and narrow streets and alleyways to get bored by. The only thing of interest is that Lenin plotted revolution in a café here. After seeing yet another unremarkable fourteenth-century basilica you too will probably be inspired to plan a violent uprising.

★ **Rynek Underground** In effect, a huge underground museum that celebrates centuries of history, literally buried under the main square. Billed as a 'journey through time' the museum is confusing and claustrophobic. This might be an archaeologist's wet dream but it's a nightmare for anyone else.

★ **Gdansk** Poland's principle seaport and a city that, when you mention its name, elicits the comment, 'Bless you.'

FIVE ABSOLUTELY TRUE FACTS ABOUT POLAND
(NONE OF WHICH WILL INSPIRE YOU TO VISIT)

★ Poland has six seasons. Apart from the usual four there are also 'early spring' and 'early winter'. In addition its alphabet consists of thirty-two letters. Greedy or what?

★ In Poland bananas are traditionally peeled from the blunt end, not the stem.

★ It has been invaded or has fought for freedom forty-three times from 1600 to 1945.

★ Beer can be served warm to ward off the intense cold.

★ Poland is the third poorest country in the EU, only being beaten by Romania and Bulgaria.

Five reasons you know you're in Poland

❶ **People will stare at you if you're even marginally different** Too short? Too tall? Too thin? Too fat? Asymmetrical haircut? Leopard print shoes? Two earrings in one earlobe? If so, expect to be gawped at like the Elephant Man. And prepare to be prodded (or possibly exhibited around the country) if you're not white.

❷ **Passengers tend to clap when Polish airliners land safely** Not surprising when you consider that since 1980 the country's national carrier, LOT Polish Airlines, has suffered seven crashes (four fatal) and seven hijackings.

❸ **Fast food portions are incredibly small** You'll need to order for two just to make sure you don't leave hungry. With this apparent rationing anyone would think there's a war on (although with Poland's turbulent history, this mentality could be excused).

❹ **There is no understanding of the term 'personal space'** Strangers feel comfortable talking to you a nose length from your face, or queuing so closely behind you that they are virtually committing a sex act.

❺ **Timings given with the same degree of accuracy as predicted by a Magic Eight Ball** Two hours ... three days ... a week ... It doesn't matter what you're told in a hotel, shop or government office. Dealing tarot cards, reading tealeaves, throwing rune stones or examining animal entrails will provide you with a greater degree of accuracy.

Useful Polish phrases

★ Cheer up. It could be worse!
  Rozweselić. Mogło być gorzej!
★ I know it might come as a surprise to you but just because I plan to
  visit Auschwitz doesn't mean I want to celebrate Third Reich ideology.
  *Wiem, że może to być zaskoczeniem dla Ciebie, ale tylko dlatego, że
  zamierzasz odwiedzić Auschwitz nie znaczy, że chcą świętować Third
  Reich ideologię.*
★ No. I do not require any building work. I am on holiday.
  Nie, nie wymaga żadnych prac budowlanych. Jestem na wakacjach.

PORTUGAL

Take from a Spaniard all his good qualities,
and there remains a Portuguese.
Spanish saying

IT'S DIFFICULT TO imagine that Portugal was once one of the genuine superpowers in the world, spearheading the exploration and colonisation of the globe and establishing some of its most lucrative trading routes. Look around the country today and your first thought is 'Really?'

Modern Portugal exhibits an unhurried approach to life that make its Spanish neighbours look like models of efficiency. The Portuguese are often described as congenial … the guidebooks' favourite euphemism for lethargic. Few people, however, know what Portugal really stands for or represents. For most people it's that 'bit on the edge of Spain' or a Brazil wannabe.

The best you can say about Portugal is that it's a country of contrasts. On the plus side it's a modern Western European nation so you don't need to worry about being chased by flies or beggars when you walk down the street. However, it also has what the guidebooks call a rural flip-side. This might sounds attractive, intriguing even … the chance to experience old-fashioned charm and the slower pace of yesteryear. In reality, however, it means a throwback to its conservative, Catholic influenced, rustic past where wearing skimpy tops or even shorts outside of towns and cities will cause widespread offence and, quite possibly, a beating.

Portugal was once home to many famous explorers who, like the Scandinavian Vikings, couldn't wait to leave the country; men like Vasco de Gama, Bartholomew Dias and Prince Henry the Navigator. These and others sailed halfway around the world. Ferdinand Magellan, however, made the rookie error of circumnavigating the globe and ended up back in Portugal.

Whatever you do, don't make the same mistake.

FADO: MUSIC FOR THE MISERABLE

The best known Portuguese music is Fado (meaning 'fate'), a traditional urban folk music characterised by high-pitched, nostalgic, bittersweet songs about lost or unrequited love, death, woe and general sadness. These are songs that are so melancholic that they make most of Leonard Cohen's back catalogue sound like 'The Laughing Policeman'.

LISBON

In 1755 a great undersea earthquake and subsequent tsunami and fires destroyed nearly all of Lisbon. The greater tragedy, however, was that the city was rebuilt. Lisbon is often described as beguiling. However, an abundance of narrow streets and alleyways are enticing only if you're a pickpocket. The Lisbon tourist office extols the virtues of the city's traditional long lunches, dinners and numerous coffee breaks. This is not so you can experience authentic Lisbon culture; it's just their way of disguising the fact there's not much else to do.

Attractions to avoid

★ **Bairro Alto** It's ironic that Bairro Alto, which translates as 'upper district', is actually home to most of Lisbon's low life. This charmless neighbourhood can be recognised by its concentration of tiny bars and expensive cafés set in narrow, rowdy, foul-smelling streets full of broken bottles and litter; a magnet for petty thieves and drug dealers. This area is also where you can observe the traditional local custom of young Portuguese men using the meandering alleyways as urinals.

★ **Tram 28** On the face of it, these vintage trams seem a charming and leisurely way to explore the city. The reality is that they're so crowded that on the rare occasion that you'll actually be able to get a seat, your only view will be the groin or backside of overweight, polyester-clad locals. Drivers have a reputation for being unhelpful and disinterested and journeys across the city are slow, jerky and nauseating.

★ **National Tile Museum** This is described as the only one of its kind in the world. Visit and you'll understand why museums devoted entirely to tiles haven't caught on in more capital cities. Think of it as a sort of bathroom showroom but a lot bigger. Here you'll see tiles from as far back as the fifteenth century; the highlight is a blue and white composition of 1,300 tiles, 75 feet in length, depicting Lisbon's cityscape. Worth a visit if you are into tiles or if you need to escape the incessant rain and wind outside (bear in mind that the Atlantic coast is considerably less placid than the Mediterranean).

PORTO

Portugal's second-largest city is described as the economic heart of the nation – albeit nowadays this is a heart clogged with the cholesterol of fiscal fear and colossal government debt. More underwhelming than even Lisbon, Porto offers even fewer reasons to visit. Attractions include a dilapidated river frontage, a tourist-infested old town, an old metal bridge and an even older church. Porto gave Port wine its name;

consuming vast quantities won't increase your enjoyment of the city but might make it slightly more bearable.

FIVE ABSOLUTELY TRUE FACTS ABOUT PORTUGAL
(NONE OF WHICH WILL INSPIRE YOU TO VISIT)

★ If you master Portuguese (and why would you?) you can also make yourself understood in Brazil, Cape Verde, Angola, Guinea Bissau, Mozambique, Principe, Sao Tome e Principe, and Equatorial Guinea.

★ You can buy a fishing licence at a bank's ATM.

★ Although matadors are not permitted to actually kill a bull during Portuguese bullfights, they can spear and lance it; a butcher kills it afterwards, safely out of sight of the crowd.

★ Portugal accounts for about 50% of the world's total cork production.

★ It's actually against the law to pee in the sea.

THE ALGARVE

Known for its crowded beaches and over-subscribed golf courses, the Algarve is the Cheryl Cole of resorts: pretty but boring.

5 reasons you know you're in Portugal

❶ **There's an almost institutionalised hatred of Brazilians** Wearing a Brazilian replica football shirt or even sporting shaved pubic hair will result in a tirade of insults that have their roots in Brazil's 1822 declaration of independence from Portugal.

❷ **Intolerance to those who can't speak Portuguese** For reasons unknown the Portuguese are incredibly proud of their language. Try to get by with Spanish and you'll be treated as a Brazilian (see above).

③ **Nativity scenes often contain a figure with his trousers around his ankles, defecating** The figure is called a 'Caganer' and has featured in Catalan culture since the late seventeenth century. In addition to the traditional Caganer design of a pooping peasant, there's been a recent tradition of it being a caricature of celebrities, athletes, historical figures, politicians and British royalty.

④ **The towns and cities are relatively uncrowded** 22% unemployment means that locals looking for work are leaving the country in droves – as many as 120,000 a year.

⑤ **You'll think you've stepped into a time warp** Central and north eastern Portugal are conspicuously underdeveloped. Here, 'quaint' means 'full of religious bigotry and insular intolerance'.

Useful Portuguese phrases

★ You've been talking to your colleague for fifteen minutes. Can you let me know when you will be able to serve me?
Você foi falar com o seu colega de 15 minutos. Você pode deixar-me saber quando você vai ser capaz de me servir?

★ Cristiano Ronaldo is rubbish and a bit gay.
Cristiano Ronaldo é lixo e um pouco gay.

★ Since when do lukewarm sardines, salted cod and peri-peri chicken constitute a diverse cuisine?
Desde quando sardinha, bacalhau e frango peri-peri constituem uma culinária diversificada?

ROMANIA

Come see our museum of the Middle Ages. We call it 'Romania.'
Conan O'Brien

ROMANIA IS A country that suffers from low self-esteem. Rather than take pride in its own merits and virtues it insists on promoting itself via comparisons with other places.

In an effort to sound glamorous it will often call itself the 'Paris of the East'. But while it does have a surly population full of its own self-importance with a questionable approach to personal hygiene and pavements strewn with dog excrement, that's where the similarity ends.

Other times it claims it's the 'Gateway to the Western Balkans' or the 'Crossroads of the Caucasus'. These descriptions are not helpful comparisons when you consider Romania is positioning itself as a stepping–off point for Albania, Armenia, Azerbaijan, the former Yugoslavia and Iran; destinations that would only feature on an itinerary of the clinically insane.

Ignore these comparisons. Romania has a lot to offer the tourist as long as the tourist wants children begging at train and bus stations, lawlessness, police corruption, unpredictability, shortages, a thriving black market economy and constant reminders of a former brutal police state.

The character of Count Dracula was inspired by the merciless Romanian prince Vlad Tepes, or Vlad the Impaler – named for his practice of punishing people by impaling them on a blunt stake forced deeply into their rectum.

Today this seems preferable to a visit to Romania.

FIVE ABSOLUTELY TRUE FACTS ABOUT ROMANIA
(NONE OF WHICH WILL INSPIRE YOU TO VISIT)

★ Europe's second worst environmental disaster (after Chernobyl) took place in 2000, when 100 tonnes of cyanide from a gold mine spilled into rivers and polluted the Danube.

★ Romania is proud of its bureaucracy and is known by locals as 'The Land of Ten Million Laws'.

★ Approximately 9,000 people a year are bitten by stray dogs.

★ There are thousands of wild bears.

★ The city of Timisoara is the birthplace of the horse tram (1869).

BUCHAREST

Beggars, officialdom, rubbish, unsightly buildings, a destroyed heritage and chaos – all legacies of the ugly face of Communism and all to be found in modern Bucharest, Romania's capital city. NB: rumours have abounded for centuries that the Romanians named their city so people would confuse it with the slightly less appalling Budapest in neighbouring Hungary; by the time tourists realised they were in the wrong place, it would be too impractical to leave.

Attractions to avoid

★ **Palace of Parliament (Palatul Poporului)** It might only be the world's second-largest building (after the Pentagon) but it's definitely the world's ugliest. The country's brutal dictator Nicolae Ceauşescu had it built as a palace but he was overthrown and executed before this vulgar landmark was completed. The ideal proof that bigger certainly does not mean better, the building remains empty, unfurnished and cold. Tours last for just over an hour and are about fifty-five minutes too long.

★ **Peasant Museum (Muzeul Taranului)** The USP of this attraction is traditional Romanian pottery, crafts, clothing and farm machinery all under one roof! Bored yet officious museum staff constantly follow visitors around to make sure they don't take photographs, however, this precaution is completely unnecessary as the authorities fail to realise that no one in their right mind would ever want to take a photo of a seventeenth-century plough.

★ **Carol Park (Liberty Park)** The only thing even remotely interesting about this park is that it was named after King Carol I, a nineteenth-century monarch who had a girl's name.

BUCHAREST TAXIS

Bucharest taxi drivers have long had a reputation for targeting and ripping off foreign tourists. This is an unfair slur on their character since they don't discriminate who they scam: tourists and locals alike are cheated and lied to with identical zeal. Although cabs display their rates on their doors these stickers should just be considered as a means of covering rust; the fact they state a price per kilometre is just a coincidence and has absolutely no bearing on the final fare. Expect surcharges for travelling during the day, at night, alone, with others, going to the airport or not going to the airport. In addition, Romanian taxi cabs are not subject to strict (or even regular) roadworthiness inspections, so expect to get in vehicles without seat belts, tyre tread or adequate braking, being driven by drivers who think nothing about turning round to talk to passengers or hand-rolling cigarettes while they drive. Some call Bucharest cabs 'idiosyncratic' or 'quirky'. A more apt description would be 'death traps'.

Other places in Romania to avoid

★ **Dracula's Castle (Transylvania):** All castle but no Dracula … The fourteenth-century Dracula's Castle, or as it's officially know, Bran Castle, is located in Transylvania in central Romania, about eighty-five miles north of Bucharest. Visitors fearing that this is a terrible tourist trap will not be disappointed. The restored castle is described as 'intriguing'; however, after spending a few minutes here you'll realise this is just a euphemism for small and uninteresting. The main disappointment, however, is that despite being promoted as the home of Dracula, there's absolutely no documented evidence that the basis of the character, Vlad the Impaler, even resided here.

Not only is Dracula probably a myth, so too are any expectations that this will be an interesting and worthwhile visit.

Did you know?

Romania's traditional sport is Oină, a bat and ball game that can be traced back to the 1360s. It's an obscure sport based on the even more obscure Russian game of lapta, with rules that can only be described as Byzantine. Imagine an interminable game of baseball, but even more incomprehensible.

Five reasons you know you're in Romania

❶ You're hungry Romanians are very proud of their cuisine, pointing out the way that it enjoys a mix of influences from surrounding countries. This is not so good when you consider Romania's neighbours are Hungary, Ukraine, Moldova, Serbia, and Bulgaria – countries that are to food as they are to space exploration.

❷ **Old men carrying goats and chickens on modern trains and buses** To the locals, this is charming or quaint. To everyone else it's noisy and unhygienic.

❸ **The pavements are covered in phlegm not gold** An occurrence that's probably linked to the high incidence of smoking (nearly half the men and a quarter of the women in Romania are regular smokers).

❹ **There are almost as many cars abandoned as driven** Not just on the sides of roads but blocking streets and the pavements ... The main Romanian car manufacturer is Dacia, a budget brand built to a price. That price is durability.

❺ **Injuries to your kidneys or spleen** Old Romanian women have no concept of the word 'queue', confusing this Western concept with that of 'stampede' or 'free-for-all'. A forceful poke in your sides with a scrawny pointy elbow or sharp umbrella tip is evidence of their dogged determination to board a bus or train before you.

USEFUL ROMANIAN PHRASES

★ Why has a 5 km taxi journey cost the equivalent of £48?
De ce a o călătorie cu taxiul costa 5 km echivalentul a 48 lire?

★ Is this your national airport or am I standing in the middle of a refugee camp?
Este acest aeroport naţional sau eu în picioare în mijlocul o tabără de refugiaţi?

★ Is there anywhere where I can get a rabies inoculation without having to fill in twenty-two different forms and queuing for several hours?
Este acolo undeva unde pot obţine o inoculare rabie, fără a fi nevoie să completaţi în 22 de diferite forme şi de aşteptare pentru câteva ore?

Advice for driving in Romania

In a word: Don't.

In six words: 'You've got to be f*cking kidding!'

Driving in Romania is so dangerous that many travel insurers put this activity in the same category as skydiving, Formula 1, cliff jumping and ostrich riding. The good news is that you'll only encounter two hazards driving in Romania. The bad news is that these two dangers are a) the roads themselves and b) the other drivers.

The roads

It's said that the Apollo astronauts practised on Romanian roads before taking their lunar buggy on to the moon's surface. Potholes the size of craters and rocks the size of boulders are not so much hazards as features. It's also difficult to know where the sides of the roads end and scrubland begins; the edge of the carriageway is usually defined by the presence of broken-down cars, stray dogs or scavenging gypsies.

The drivers

Over-confident, aggressive and imbecilic. Romanian drivers are all these and more. In this case the 'more' includes hostile and psychotic. Drive in the cities and you'll experience a sense of machismo that would rival that seen on the set of *The Expendables*. Each 'give way' and 'stop sign' is viewed by Romanian men as a 'girlie inconvenience', while failing to beat a red light or travelling more than a turnip length behind the car in front shows a complete lack of testosterone. In what is more a physics experiment than an example of sensible road craft, you'll also notice the locals continually attempt to prove that it is possible to go faster than the speed of light.

The only time you'll see drivers travelling slowly is when they're in one of the innumerable horse and carts that travel on narrow rural roads, holding you up and adding the heady waft of manure to your frustration. Note to the Romanian Tourist Ministry: these horse and carts do not make your country look like a 'living museum'. They make it look like a land of rag and bone merchants.

SKI EUROPE!
(OR DON'T)

CONSIDER THE EUROPEAN ski resorts of Verbier, Val d'Isere, Courchevel, Kitzbühel and Chamonix. Despite ski-passes that cost the same as two months' council tax and après-ski drinks that redefine the word exorbitant, most people still visit these resorts in the mistaken belief that they're going somewhere exotic and glamorous; places where they'll be rubbing shoulders and ski-poles with minor European royalty – and by some weird type of osmosis, absorbing thousands of years of in-breeding and assumed sophistication in the process.

The reality is somewhat different …

Totally annoying groups of people you'll meet on a European skiing holiday

★ Hordes of smug middle management from Munich or Düsseldorf, wearing ski wear that's as brightly coloured as they are overweight. They think they have the ski skills and charisma of Jean-Claude Killy. The reality is that they have the ski skills and charisma of Jean-Claude Van Damme.

★ Ridiculously handsome Swiss ski-instructors who prey on desperately romantic wives trapped in long, loveless marriages.

★ Pretentious yet rugged hard-core French skiers who hold court with the women by telling them, 'I tell zee mountains my problems. Zey are good listeners.'

* Swarms of eight-year-old Austrian children who demonstrate the same level of confidence and fervour as members of the Hitler Youth.
* Proficient German skiers who view you less as a human being and more as a slalom gate.
* Loud, ebullient teenage Italian snowboarders who use the words 'phat', 'tight' and 'fakie' and who'll make you feel even more inadequate and older than you are.
* A chalet cook whose only qualification for the job seems to be a two-year stint in the Grenoble branch of Nandos.

RUDE-SOUNDING
EUROPEAN PLACE NAMES

YOU MIGHT ALREADY know that Sweden has a Slut or that there's a Minge in Belgium, but here is a full list of European place names that are as rude as they are real:

★ Clit, Romania
★ Condom, France
★ C*nt, Spain
★ Feces de Abaixo (Lower Feces), Spain
★ Fjuckby, Sweden
★ Fucking, Austria
★ Horn, Austria
★ Horn, Iceland
★ Labia, Belgium
★ Minge, Belgium
★ Minge, Lithuania

★ Oberfucking, Austria
★ Pis, Spain
★ Pis, France
★ Semen, Moldova
★ Semen, Bulgaria
★ Slut, Sweden
★ Spurt, Belgium
★ Stiff, France
★ Tös, Germany
★ Turdo, Romania
★ Wank, Germany
★ Wankum, Germany

SLOVAKIA AND SLOVENIA

 NOWN AS THE Jedward of Europe, hardly anyone can tell these two countries apart and fewer actually care.

SPAIN

A wonderful country where there are only three things
in excess: fleas, bed-bugs and Spaniards.
Victor Hugo

HOW TIMES HAVE changed. Once Spain was the most popular package holiday destination and an exotic location for Brits whose most cosmopolitan experience up until then was watching the Eurovision Song Contest. Nowadays the weak euro and the freefalling Spanish economy have made the country far less attractive for tourists. Many British holidaymakers have abandoned Spain for Turkey and it must be said that losing out in the popularity stakes to a third world nation is a major indictment of the condition of your own country.

But look beyond a sovereign state set to follow Greece and Cyprus in an inevitable slide into a calamitous fiscal abyss and you'll see a nation rich in history and tradition but with a fresh, modern outlook on life. A country with a kaleidoscope of landscapes from beaches, to sunburnt plains and mountain peaks. A country that combines technology and a very modern infrastructure with the highest levels of disorganisation, lethargy, incompetence and a questionable understanding of the word 'productivity'.

Yes, Spain is truly a land of contrasts; it's where an industrialised nation meets a banana republic.

MADRID

If Madrid were a suspect in an identity parade no witness would be able to pick it out. As capital cities go it's anonymous, bland and anodyne. If it were a flavour it would be vanilla. If it were a comedian it would be Michael McIntyre. As landmarks go, Rome has the Colosseum, Paris has the Eiffel Tower and even Athens has the Acropolis. What does Madrid have? Nothing. Or as the Spanish say, '*nada*'. Sure, there are museums and plazas, a park and even a stone arch but nothing remotely memorable. Once you've seen one baroque municipal building you've seen them all. In lieu of any recognisable landmarks however, Madrid does have a reputation as being the most frustrating European capital city to drive in. Its central location within Spain means that all roads literally do lead to Madrid. This can account for the traffic jams that start in the morning rush hour and finish four hours after midnight.

Attractions to avoid

There's a park, a royal palace, a square, a fountain, some museums, a cathedral and a statue of Christopher Columbus (who wasn't even Spanish). None of these are worth describing in detail and even fewer are worth a visit.

BARCELONA

Located on the Mediterranean in the northeast corner of Spain, Barcelona is the capital of Catalonia, a region with its own culture and language that likes to think of itself as being independent from the rest of the country. The people in this area generally confuse pride with arrogance, which might account for the widespread rudeness and lack of courtesy from most of the locals. If you do visit Barcelona be prepared to be ignored by waiters, argued with by public transport employees, insulted by shop assistants or given the finger by hotel staff.

The Barcelona tourist office claims its city can keep you occupied for weeks but that's mainly because malicious locals will give you wrong directions on purpose and spiteful taxi drivers will always take you the long way round or drop you off miles from your destination.

Attractions to avoid

★ **La Sagrada Família** Guidebooks describe the Church of the Sacred Family as 'a magical structure' and 'an overwhelming masterpiece'. However, more accurate descriptions are 'tourist infested building site' and 'ill-conceived pastiche'. This cathedral is universally heralded as a masterpiece of Antoni Gaudi's engineering and architectural skills. However, the fact that it was started in 1882 and is still under construction could be seen as a testament to the general laziness and lack of productivity of Spanish builders.

★ **Nou Camp** If you love football, badly organised tours, wasting almost €25 and looking at vast amounts of concrete, you'll enjoy a visit to FC Barcelona's stadium.

★ **Magic Fountain** The biggest ornamental fountain in Barcelona features streams of dancing and cascading water, synchronised with atmospheric music and lights. Well, it does if it's actually working. From Mondays to Thursdays it's usually closed for maintenance and on weekends it tends to be beset by mechanical problems. Fridays? That's the day that someone usually forgets to turn it on.

TORREMOLINOS AND FUENGIROLA (COSTA DEL SOL)
BENIDORM (COSTA BLANCA)

Sun, sea, sand, sangria and San Miguel ... Since the 1970s these three resorts have provided many young visitors not just with their first experience of a foreign holiday, but also their first experience of having to attend an STI clinic when they returned.

For many years these resorts enjoyed a reputation for half-built hotels, inattentive staff, all-day breakfasts, English-themed pubs, drunken men wearing 'Lads on Tour' T-shirts, singing football songs by the pool, drunken women the colour of lobsters with large tattoos and even larger deposits of cellulite, and chips with everything. Nowadays it's a completely different story; there are far fewer half-built hotels.

Five reasons you know you're in Spain

❶ **It's noisy** Most Spaniards confuse talking with shouting, a situation exacerbated by the fact that they are incapable of having a conversation unless they are standing at least six feet apart or, more often, on opposite sides of the street.

❷ **Levels of bureaucracy that make the pre-perestroika Soviet civil service resemble a slick, well-oiled machine** An encounter with Spanish officialdom would be enough to make even the Dalai Lama want to punch someone in the face. If you actually manage to find one, government offices in Spain only open at certain times on certain days of the week and by the time you've reached the front of the serpentine queue the various regulations would have changed so you'll have to go back and complete a whole different set of forms and paperwork. The whole process can be compared to trying to walk up an Escher staircase.

❸ **Fireworks any time of the day or night** Although traditionally used to herald the start or finish (or any point in the middle) of fiesta celebrations, the Spanish need no excuse to set off fireworks. With displays that eschew spectacle for loud noise and random explosions that resemble underground nuclear testing, any visit to Spain combines breathtaking spectacle with insomnia. Those suffering from Post Traumatic Stress Disorder are advised not to travel.

❹ **Frustration over opening times** Most businesses are closed between 2 p.m. and 5 p.m. (6 p.m. in some areas) so their employees can take an afternoon nap in the heat. This tradition is only practised in Spain and Hispanic countries; hotter countries seem to manage without it. The Spanish call this a 'siesta'. Everyone else calls it laziness.

❺ **It's no fun being a vegetarian** Most Spanish meals combine meat with three other meats.

FIVE ABSOLUTELY TRUE FACTS ABOUT SPAIN
(NONE OF WHICH WILL INSPIRE YOU TO VISIT)

★ In many Spanish bars and taverns, throwing dirty napkins, olive pits and ham fat on the floor is commonplace and considered acceptable.

★ Over the last ten years the average cost of living has risen by 31% in real terms. During the last year alone staple food prices have risen by 48% to 115%.

★ In July 2012 the British Embassy in Madrid reported a 10% rise in British tourists being ambushed on Spanish roads.

★ There is no tooth fairy in Spain; instead there's a tooth mouse called Ratoncito Perez (not good if you're scared of mice. Or losing teeth).

★ Spain is not renowned for its inventors but it did give the world the mop.

A guide to Spanish culture

★ **Flamenco** Not so much a traditional Andalusian gypsy dance, more an excuse to look surly and shuffle around, banging your feet on the floor. Flamenco is Spanish for 'spoilt child'.

★ **Spanish Art** The three most famous exponents were Miró, Picasso and Salvador Dalí. Miró had a girl's name (Joan) and drew geometric squiggles, Picasso thought that women had both eyes on the side of their head, while Dalí thought that placing a lobster on a telephone was clever. Innovative, ground-breaking geniuses or just care-in-the-community patients? It's a fine line.

★ **Bullfighting** Known in Spanish as *Corrida de Toros*, this phrase translates literally as 'waving a curtain and stabbing animals with a pointy stick'. Critics deny that this is a real sport, instead viewing it as a demonstration of epic levels of barbaric cruelty. Supporters claim it is a valid and historic Spanish tradition. However, that description could equally be applied to the Inquisition.

★ **Don Quixote** In a 2002 a survey of 100 of the world's best authors declared this book by Miguel de Cervantes to be 'the best book of all time'. Praise indeed. However, it should noted that the study is now of questionable value, as it was conducted before the publication of *Harry Potter and the Half-Blood Prince*.

★ **Paella** A Spanish dish that was created just to make use of leftovers.

Useful phrases to use in Spain

★ Didn't I see you on *Crimewatch*? The one where they recreated the 1983 Brink's-MAT robbery?
¿No te he ver en Crimewatch? En el que se recrea el 1983 Brink's-MAT robo?

★ I am trying to have a quiet drink. I do not want to hear about your country's 26% overall unemployment, 55% youth unemployment, massive levels of personal debt, crippling inflation, downgrading of banks and €100bn of rescue loans.
Estoy tratando de tomar una copa tranquila. No quiero oír hablar de un 26% de desempleo general de su país, el 55% de desempleo juvenil, los niveles masivos de deuda personal, la inflación paralizante, degradación de los bancos y €100 mil millones de préstamos de rescate.

★ I'm sorry to hear that your pool cleaning/gardening/hairdressing business failed but please stop bothering me with your tale of shattered dreams.
Lamento escuchar que su piscina limpieza/jardinería/peluquería negocio fracasó, pero por favor deja de molestarme con su relato de los sueños rotos.

PEOPLE SAY THE NICEST THINGS ABOUT SPAIN . . .

Spain would be a fine country, if there were no Spaniards in it.
German saying

In Spanish inns they use the same oil for the lamps, soups and salads.
Algernon Swinburne

The Spaniard is a bad servant, but a worse master.
English saying

He who would eat in Spain must bring his kitchen along.
German saying

The only good thing that comes from the east is the sun.
Portugese saying

A country that has sold its soul for cement and petrol,
and can only be saved by a series of earthquakes.
Cyril Connolly

A Spaniard may be trusted – but no further than your nose.
German saying

A Spaniard and a braggart are the same thing.
German saying

The Spaniards teach the Germans to steal, while the Germans
teach the Spaniards to gorge and swill.
German saying

A Spaniard is no Spaniard if he is not a snob.
German saying

All Spaniards have sticky fingers. In past centuries, the pots
on the stove would have padlocks on them.
German saying

The Spaniard is a Frenchman turned inside out.
German saying

SWEDEN

Speculation is that the Swedes are slowly boring themselves to death.
This is certainly the case if their cars and movies are any indication.

P. J. O'Rourke

IT MIGHT HAVE been France that came up with the concept of *laissez faire* but it's Sweden that is its greatest advocate. Laid back to the point of being horizontal, Sweden is a carefree country with a relaxed take on almost everything from sex to sandwiches (a policy of openness applies to both). If Sweden were a person, nothing would phase it; it would just sigh, shrug its shoulders and say 'meh'.

Proof of Sweden's extreme liberalism can be seen in its tolerance of things as hazardous to the country as nuclear power and McDonald's restaurants; per capita Sweden has the highest number of nuclear power plants *and* McDonald's in Europe. Less dangerous, but equally contentious, is their relaxed attitude towards fashion. Like the Brontosaurus, 80s fashion trends died out for a reason but in Sweden it's like the decade never went away. The Swedes still embrace long fluorescent sleeveless T-shirts, chunky belts, spandex and leg warmers. They call it retro. Everyone else calls it 'looking like a *Flashdance* twat'.

For the tourist, however, the most frustrating aspect of the country's chilled approach to life comes from what's known in Swedish as *'lagom'*. Described as the very essence of Swedishness (apart from pickled herring), the word roughly translates as 'just the right amount; not too much or not too little'.

The result of a long adherence to this ethos is a country that's extremely average in terms of being interesting, appealing or even engaging.

THE LAND OF THE MIDNIGHT SUN: DON'T GO … IT'LL MESS WITH YOUR HEAD

Within the Swedish Arctic Circle, between the end of May and mid-July, the sun is visible for twenty-four hours. At first this will be a novelty and visitors are encouraged to play golf, go white water rafting, skiing or even mountain climbing in the region – taking advantage of the fact that it's always daytime. However, not experiencing night for long periods of time can cause hypomania, a condition characterised by persistent and intense mood swings.

The opposite occurs in winter with a phenomenon called Polar Nights; two or three months of darkness that can trigger bouts of deep depression leading to a significant increase in suicides. The number of practising psychiatrists in the region has been steadily increasing year on year. Now you know why.

STOCKHOLM

When any city is described as a 'quintessential European capital' it's because there's absolutely nothing else positive to say about it … i.e. it offers no landmarks or attractions of any note. Such it is with Stockholm. Visitors often describe their experience as horrifyingly upsetting or traumatic but still manage to show positive feelings towards the city; emotions considered highly irrational in light of their harrowing time spent there. Psychologists call this phenomenon 'the Stockholm syndrome'.

Attractions to avoid

★ **Vasa Ship Museum** The *Vasa* was a prestigious Swedish warship that was far too top-heavy. This resulted in it sinking on its maiden voyage in 1628 before it had even left Stockholm harbour. Rather than be embarrassed by the sheer incompetence of its dim-witted shipbuilders, the Swedes have put the preserved wreck on display. The museum is relatively small so expect a chaotic time in crowded conditions with tour guides shouting over one another to be heard. It might not seem like it but there are marginally better ways to spend an afternoon in Stockholm than looking at the remains of an old boat.

★ **The Old Town** An over-crowded tourist-infested parody of a European Old Town that could be anywhere. Old Palace? Tick. Mediaeval church? Tick. Restored cobblestone streets and narrow alleyways? Tick. Restaurants high in price and low in charm? Tick. Complete over-commercialisation? Tick. Avoid at all costs? Tick.

★ **Skeppsholmen** A small island in the middle of Stockholm and home to a church, a modern art museum and museum of architecture. The public restrooms are quite clean with powerful hand dryers; this is the most complimentary thing one can say about this destination.

★ **Royal Palace (Kungliga Slottet)** The highlight of a visit here is not the drab royal apartments or the museum filled with replicas of precious objects; it's the daily changing of the guard. With the accompaniment of a military band, this resembles a flag-waving dance routine more suited to *The X-Factor* than any form of precision marching.

PICKLED HERRING: IS IT AN APPETIZER OR A WAY OF LIFE?

Alongside IKEA, Volvo, ABBA and nubile au pairs, Sweden is closely associated with pickled herring; expect to see it on every single menu in a variety of forms. It's said that pickled herring to the Swedes is like chocolate for everyone else. That comparison fails to acknowledge that chocolate isn't slimy with a disgusting pungent fishy/vinegary smell.

> ## DID YOU KNOW?
>
> ★ It's forbidden to wear a swimming costume at any public sauna in Sweden.
> ★ A Swede, Gideon Sundbäck, perfected the design of the zip. (It is unknown whether the motivation for this development was the need to remove clothes quickly, an imperative driven by the burgeoning Swedish soft porn industry).

Other places in Sweden to avoid

★ **The Volvo Museum, Gothenburg** *The* place to see not just the history of Volvo cars but also Volvo trucks, buses, marine engines and construction equipment. One guidebook described the museum as 'intriguing, remarkable and incredibly stimulating' and 'the ultimate must-see attraction on any visit to Sweden'. All copies of this guidebook were soon pulped and the editor slapped around the face then summarily dismissed.

★ **The Icehotel, Jukkasjärvi** Located in the north of the country, about 125 miles within the Arctic Circle, your first clue that the Icehotel might not be as hospitable as it sounds is the fact that it's used by the Swedish Army for Arctic survival training. The hotel itself is constructed purely out of snow and ice with beds being blocks of compacted snow covered with reindeer hide, and furniture carved from blocks of ice. This sounds like a memorable, if not quirky, place to stay until you realise that the temperature in your room is likely to be about –5°C, meaning you'll find it far too cold to sleep, of if you do, there's a chance you'll die in the night from hypothermia.

★ **Orsa Bjornpark, Grönklitt** Located about 170 miles northwest of Stockholm, this is the biggest bear park in Europe. Brown bears wander freely about the forested park, which is also home to polar bears, Siberian tigers, snow leopards, wolves and wolverines. The organisers claim there is something for everyone. This includes a tasty meal for the predators if anyone slips off the icy viewing platforms or precarious walkways.

FIVE ABSOLUTELY TRUE FACTS ABOUT SWEDEN
(NONE OF WHICH WILL INSPIRE YOU TO VISIT)

★ Approximately 20% of the country's police stations close during the summer on the basis that most people are on holiday.

★ It's traditional to go trick or treating at Easter.

★ You can only buy alcohol at state-run off-licences called Systembolaget and these close at 6 p.m. during the week and at 2 p.m. on Saturdays.

★ Most shops and restaurants close for an entire month in the summer (usually July).

★ Each year approximately 4,500 moose collide with vehicles on Swedish roads.

Five reasons you know you're in Sweden

❶ **You'll notice that the locals have a limited range of facial expressions** Two in fact: 'smiling' or 'blank'.

❷ **No matter how carefully it's arranged or presented, the food always looks like leftovers** *Smörgåsbord* is Swedish for 'a platter full of cold things you won't want to eat'.

❸ **You'll get used to seeing a sign that says 'Stängt' (Closed)** Most shops and stores shut at 6 p.m. (7 p.m. for late night opening).

❹ **Everyone whines about the weather** It's as if Swedes have never ever experienced freezing temperatures, heavy snowfall or the fact that it's dark and cold for three months. We know the weather there sucks; stop reminding us.

⑤ **It's like going into Argos every time you shop** Even if there's no apparent queue you still have to take a number from a machine and await your turn to be served in nearly all shops, post offices, chemists, train stations, doctors and banks.

USEFUL SWEDISH PHRASES

★ Is this authentic Swedish beer or have you flavoured your pee with hops?
Detta är äkta svenskt öl eller har du smaksatt urinen med humle?

★ Please put some clothes on. I feel uncomfortable with your nakedness.
Vänligen klä på. Jag känner dig obekväm med din nakenhet.

★ Mmmm! Twenty-four varieties of pickled herrings. You spoil me!
Mmmm! Tjugofyra sorter av kryddsillen. Du skämmer bort mig!

THE SYMBOLISM
OF THE EUROPEAN FLAG

IN 1985 THE European flag was adopted by all EU leaders as the official emblem of the European Union; since then, however, it's become representative of Europe's identity in a much wider sense. It consists of a dark blue background and twelve golden stars arranged in a circle. Gold represents the colour of urine and symbolises the billions of pounds that have been flushed down the toilet as a result of the Common Agricultural Policy.

The meaning of the stars

The twelve stars each represent one of the core principles of the EU:

- Interference
- Bureaucracy
- Duplicity
- Dishonesty
- Unaccountability
- Treachery
- Intrusion
- Autocracy
- Federalism
- Subsidisation
- Inefficiency
- Deficit

THE EU

Countries joining the European Union are akin to middle-aged
couples with failing marriages meeting in a darkened
hotel room in Brussels for a group grope.

Anonymous

THE EUROPEAN UNION. Three words that carry the exact same
appeal as 'Madonna's new single', 'starring Hugh Grant' or 'with
extra tofu'.

Unwieldy, undemocratic and unloved, the EU is the post-war bastard
child of Nazis and Vichy turncoats. Starting with the Treaty of Rome
and continuing throughout its various insidious incarnations, the EU
has seduced member countries by promising them prosperity and
political stability, while systematically eradicating their sovereignty in
order to create a single entity; one where an unelected über civil service
dictates and controls the lives of every European citizen. This is an
ambition that goes by a number of names including a Federal Europe,
the United States of Europe or Third Time Lucky for Germany.

In 1973 the UK joined the EU (then known as the EEC) in order to
ensure a free trade agreement with member states. In return it's given up
a significant part of its autonomy to a bullying, deceitful, evil, despotic
bureaucracy.

Faust made a better deal.

Ten myths perpetuated by the EU

❶ The EU engenders peace and harmony within member states

Really? High inflation, tax rises, job cuts, loss of pensions and meteoric rises in unemployment have caused massive unrest and widespread violent protests from Lisbon to Nicosia. What part of 'harmony' doesn't the EU understand?

❷ EU officials are dynamic policy makers who implement progressive directives and regulations

Really? Brussels bureaucrats redefine the words 'bland' and 'faceless'. If they were an ice cream flavour they wouldn't even be vanilla; instead they'd be the scoop festering at the bottom of the bowl of dirty, lukewarm water.

❸ The EU is only concerned with legislation that is integral to the wellbeing of European citizens

Really? It is concerned with passing laws that are as arcane as they are extreme. On one hand EU legislation grants unwarranted human rights to convicted terrorists; on the other it defines the acceptable curvature of bananas and cucumbers. Go figure.

❹ The EU believes in fairness, equality and open justice

Really? In the UK you are considered innocent until proven guilty. This principle is abhorrent to EU lawmakers, whose European Arrest Warrant means that you can be accused of a crime in one country and extradited without trial, purely on the basis of someone filling in forms correctly. As Ian Hislop, editor of *Private Eye*, once famously said, 'If that's justice, then I'm a banana' (although under EU law, not a very curved one).

⑤ **A centralised EU Commission means huge savings in the running of government**

Really? The EU often confuses the phrase 'huge savings' with 'colossal waste'. For starters, it spends over €5 million each year on chauffeured limousines to transport MEPs around Strasbourg. Then there's the twenty official recognised languages and 380 language permutations within the EU, which means that Brussels spends more than €1 billion each year on translation and interpretation services.

And that's 'squandering tax payers' money' in any language.

⑥ **All EU funded projects are carefully vetted and considered in order to provide the best value for European citizens**

Really? Recent handouts included £660,000 to Brazil to fund a project concerned with the 'social integration of women living in fishing villages', £240,000 to Russia for an arts project in St Petersburg entitled 'Listening to Architecture', almost £50,000 to create a 'European hip-hop laboratory' in Lyon, France ... and don't forget £1.8 million spent on offices and a luxury hotel and apartment complex to house EU officials in that frantic hub of European political action ... Barbados.

⑦ **The EU is democratic**

Really? Members of the European Commission are not elected by the voting public yet they can introduce policies that individual national governments are legally bound to undertake even though they weren't part of their own election manifesto. Even Pol Pot or Genghis Khan would have felt slightly awkward about wielding that degree of power.

⑧ **Most citizens have a deep-rooted interest in European politics and want to actively engage with EU decision makers**

Really? Can you name more than one MEP? Have you ever voted in a European election? Do you know the difference between the

European Parliament, the European Council and the European Commission? Do you understand the significance of the Treaty of Paris, the Treaty of Rome or the Maastricht Treaty? Can you name the country that currently holds the EU presidency? Do you give a rat's arse?

⑨ **Executive members of the EU governing body have always acted responsibly and conscientiously, working for the greater good of Europe** Really? In 1999, all twenty European commissioners resigned after claims of mass fraud and corruption. The official independent report at the time stated that none of the commissioners 'had the slightest sense of responsibility'.

⑩ **A fixed exchange system, common monetary policy and price transparency make the Euro a robust and appropriate currency** Really?